THE MONKEY AND THE WAY OF ZEN

A TRANSFORMATIONAL JOURNEY IN 28 SHORT STORIES

SERENA CHOO

SISPARA HODFORD

Copyright © 2025 by Serena Choo.

All rights reserved. The content contained within this book may not be reproduced, duplicated or transmitted without direct written permission from the author or the publisher.

Under no circumstances will any blame or legal responsibility be held against the publisher, or author, for any damages, reparation, or monetary loss due to the information contained within this book, either directly or indirectly.

LEGAL NOTICE

This book is copyright protected. It is only for personal use. You cannot amend, distribute, sell, use, quote or paraphrase any part, or the content within this book, without the consent of the author or publisher.

DISCLAIMER

Please note the information contained within this document is for educational and entertainment purposes only. The content within this book has been derived from various sources and all effort has been executed to present accurate, up to date, reliable, complete information. It is the intent of the author to provide general knowledge and helpful information on the subjects discussed to assist readers in their search for greater understanding and use of the ideas, thoughts, and principles presented. The advice and strategies contained herein may not be suitable for your situation. No warranties of any kind are declared or implied. Readers acknowledge that the author is not engaged in the rendering of professional advice. Please consult a licensed professional before attempting any of the exercises in this book.

By reading this document, the reader agrees that under no circumstances is the author responsible for any losses, direct or indirect, that are incurred as a result of the use of the information contained within this document, including, but not limited to, errors, omissions, or inaccuracies.

ISBN-13: 978-0-9545974-8-1 (Paperback)
ISBN-13: 978-0-9545974-9-8 (Hardcover)

Contents

An Invitation	V
Prologue	VII
1. The Lens of Perception	1
2. The Veil of Separation	5
3. Returning to the Self	10
4. The Quiet Magic of Trust	14
5. The Stories We Weave	18
6. Everything Echoes	24
7. The Joy of No Agenda	29
8. Relax Into Receiving	35
9. The Body's Quiet Wisdom	41
10. Life Unfolding for You	45
11. The Art of Active Waiting	48
12. The Spiral Path of Growth	52
13. Responding, Not Reacting	57
14. The Hidden Gift of Synchronicity	61
15. Boredom: A Doorway to Insight	65
16. The Wild Freedom of No Goals	71

17. The Flow of Having Enough	75
18. The Paradox of Striving	81
19. The Weightless Freedom of Letting Go	87
20. The Gentle Wisdom of Not Knowing	93
21. The Space Between Stories	98
22. The Boundless Lightness of Being	103
23. The Stories We Weave (Revisited)	108
24. The Power of Accepting What Is	112
25. Trusting the Timing	117
26. Beyond Judgment and Duality	121
27. Becoming Empty	127
28. The Dance of Sovereignty	132
Stay A Moment Longer	137
Share Your Reflection	138
A Note From the Author: Where This Book Meets Buddhist Psychology	139
About the Author	140
Book Club Guide	141

An Invitation

Come, sit for a while.

There is no rush. No urgency.

You do not need to chase. You do not need to fix anything. You do not need to become more than you already are.

For so long, the mind has been searching—racing forward, tangled in worries, grasping at certainty. It looks for peace as if it were something distant, just beyond reach.

But what if peace and happiness were never something to be found?

What if they are already here—hidden beneath the noise of thinking, waiting to be seen?

If you find yourself trapped in overthinking, stress, or striving, these stories offer a different way forward. Each one is a gentle interruption—a pause in the mind's endless loops, an opening for something deeper to emerge.

Zen wisdom is not about gaining knowledge. It is about dissolving what is unnecessary. For centuries, Zen masters have shared short, paradoxical tales, known as koans—not to explain the truth, but to point toward it.

While traditional Zen koans often use paradox to break through conditioned thinking, these Zen-inspired stories are written with a gentler approach—offering reflections that invite awareness in narrative form.

Let these stories settle in your mind. Read them once, then again later. Notice how different passages speak to you at different times. The story that means little today may unlock something profound when you least expect it—a day, a month, even years from now.

Read. Let go. See what arises.

At the end of each story, you will find a short Pause & Reflect prompt. These are not instructions, but gentle invitations—to turn inward, to notice, to simply be aware.

So take a breath.

And allow yourself to see what has always been.

Prologue

The monkey was always moving. His feet never stayed on a single branch for long, his thoughts never rested in one place. He swung from tree to tree, always chasing something—though he could never say exactly what.

A sense of unease followed him, like a shadow he could not escape.

His mind was restless, spinning with questions, worries, doubts. He was quick to anger when things didn't go his way, impatient when answers didn't come fast enough, frustrated when the world refused to bend to his will. The harder he tried to control things, the more complicated everything seemed to become.

And yet, despite all his effort, despite all his running, he felt no closer to peace.

At night, as he lay on a high branch staring at the stars, the weight of his own thoughts pressed down on him. He longed for something more—a life that was not an endless chase, a mind that did not feel like a tangled jungle of overthinking.

But how?

Where would he find what he was looking for?

Not that he even knew what that was.

One evening, as the jungle settled into its familiar rhythm of rustling leaves and distant hoots, the monkey sat among his troop, watching the others groom and chatter. The branches swayed under their playful movements, but his own limbs felt restless.

A younger monkey swung past him, hooting loudly before dropping onto a nearby branch. "Why do you always look like you swallowed a sour berry?"

The others chuckled.

"Do you ever wonder if there's more than this?" he asked, his voice quieter than usual.

One of the older monkeys, his fur speckled with silver, drawled sarcastically. "More than what? More than climbing, eating, and napping?"

A lanky monkey, still hanging upside down from a nearby vine, snorted. "Careful, or you'll end up like the bat! Always hanging upside down, thinking strange thoughts."

The troop burst into laughter.

The monkey's tail flicked irritably. "I just mean... don't you ever feel like something is missing?" He hesitated, then tried again. "Like you're running, but you don't know where?"

Another monkey stretched lazily across a thick branch, yawning. "You think too much. If you stopped climbing trees to chase thoughts, maybe you'd be happier."

A smaller monkey, still half-grooming his friend's fur, smirked. "Or maybe he just needs a mate. That's what's missing."

More laughter.

The monkey clenched his jaw, heat rising in his chest. It wasn't just the teasing—it was that they didn't care. Every day felt the same. Every conversation predictable. And yet, when he tried to speak of it, he was met with jokes and dismissive grins.

No one ever wondered about the things that kept him awake at night. No one ever seemed to feel what he felt—the aching, restless feeling that there had to be something more.

PROLOGUE

That night, as the others curled up together, he climbed higher into the canopy, perching alone beneath the vast stretch of sky. The stars shimmered like scattered seeds across an endless field. Somewhere beyond this jungle, beyond the life he had always known, something waited for him.

One day, he heard a rumor.

Somewhere beyond the dense jungle, past the river that ran like silver in the moonlight, there was a master. A teacher who spoke of things beyond what the monkey had ever known.

Some said the master had the answers to everything. Others said he simply pointed the way.

The monkey scoffed when he first heard the tale. A single master, holding the key to everything he had spent his whole life searching for? Foolishness.

And yet... the idea would not leave him.

What if this master had what he was looking for?

But what if he left everything behind, made the long journey, only to find nothing? What if he returned home empty-handed, laughed at, a fool?

Doubt twisted in his chest.

But he had to know.

And so, one morning, before the sun had fully risen, the monkey left the only life he had ever known. He followed the whisper of a rumor, chasing a master who might not even exist, searching for something he could not yet name.

And from that moment on, he was no longer just a monkey.

He became the wandering monkey.

Chapter 1
The Lens of Perception

The wandering monkey had spent many days traveling through the dense jungle, following rumors of a wise master who lived in the mountains. The sun burned hot above him, beads of sweat dampening his fur. Tangled vines tugged at his limbs, as if the very forest wanted to hold him back from his quest. Yet, he pressed on, for he carried a question heavier than his aching limbs: *Why is life so difficult?*

When he finally arrived at the old temple, his expectations shattered. No grand halls, no golden statues—just an elderly master sitting beside a simple pond, his gaze fixed on the rippling water. The stillness of the place felt unsettling, as if the air itself held its breath.

His nose wrinkled. *Was this the master that many spoke of?*

He had imagined someone... more. Someone who looked wise. Someone who carried an air of importance. Instead, this was just an old man in plain robes, silent and still as a rock.

The monkey shifted from foot to foot, waiting. Had the master even noticed him?

After what felt like an eternity, he cleared his throat. "Master, I have traveled far seeking wisdom. My mind is full of thoughts, doubts, and worries. The world is unfair. People misunderstand me. No matter what I do, things seem to work against me. I want to see things clearly, to understand what is true."

Under his breath, he muttered, "You don't even look like the master I heard of."

The old man finally lifted his gaze, studying the monkey's weary face for a long moment before reaching into his robes. Without a word, he pulled out a small, polished bronze mirror and held it up.

"What do you see?"

The monkey frowned, ears twitching. His fur was matted from the journey, his eyes heavy with exhaustion, his face tense. "I see myself."

"And now?" asked the master, tilting the mirror slightly.

The monkey squinted. Now, in the reflection, he could see the temple behind him.

"I see the temple too."

Then the master dipped the mirror into the pond. The water shimmered as the monkey's reflection twisted into strange, warped shapes.

His stomach clenched. He leaned forward, staring hard. His face looked monstrous. His eyes bulged, his mouth twisted sideways, his fur blurred into strange patterns.

He recoiled, suddenly uneasy. "This—this isn't right!" he snapped, shaking his head. "I don't look like that!"

The master said nothing, simply letting the ripples settle. The monkey glanced at him sharply, his tail lashing in agitation. *Was this a joke? A trick?*

But as the water stilled, his real face returned.

The master finally spoke, his voice calm. "Your reflection changes depending on what you look through. A mirror, a pond, a still or disturbed mind—each presents a different image. Tell me, which reflection is the real one?"

The monkey knitted his brows together. "I suppose... none of them?"

The master nodded. "What you see is always shaped by what you look through. The world is not as it is—it is as you are. When your mind is still, you see clearly. When it is disturbed, you see distortions. If you believe the distortions, you suffer."

The monkey let out a sharp breath, his shoulders sagging. He kicked a small stone into the pond, watching the ripples spread. "So... if I see unfairness, suffering, and obstacles, does that mean they aren't real?"

The master stood and gestured toward the mountains in the distance. "Tell me, do you see that mountain?"

The monkey nodded.

"How does the mountain look from here?"

"Small," the monkey admitted.

"And if you stood in the valley, looking up?"

"It would seem massive," the monkey said.

The master nodded. "And if clouds covered its peak?"

"Then I wouldn't see it at all."

The master's eyes twinkled. "And yet, the mountain remains."

The monkey opened his mouth, then closed it again, without speaking.

"Perception shapes experience," the master said. "But reality does not change because you see it differently. What changes is your experience of it."

The monkey rubbed his arms. "Then... how do I know what is true?"

The master lifted the mirror again, this time tilting it toward the sky. The glass reflected the open expanse of blue above. "When you stop looking for yourself in every reflection, the world appears as it is. Truth is not found in the distortions of perception but in the stillness that remains when the mind is clear."

The monkey sat for a long time, watching the pond return to stillness. The wind whispered through the trees, carrying with it the gentle rustling of leaves and the scent of damp earth and jasmine. He did not argue, did not try to grasp the lesson all at once.

For the first time in his life, he did not try to answer—he simply observed.

And in that silence, something within him shifted.

Pause & Reflect

How has your perception shaped your reality in the past? Can you think of a time when changing your perspective transformed how you felt about a situation?

Chapter 2
The Veil of Separation

The wandering monkey woke the next morning, still tired from his travels. He stretched, his limbs stiff from the uneven ground, and rubbed his face with both hands. His mind immediately went into overdrive, replaying his meeting with the master the day before. It had all made sense then, but now, in the cold light of morning, he wasn't so sure.

His tail twitched as uncertainty crept in. *What if that wasn't even the real master?*

He kicked at a loose pebble, his frustration rising, when a voice behind him interrupted his spiraling thoughts.

"You're new here, aren't you?"

The monkey whipped around. A young temple student stood nearby, his simple robes lightly dusted with dirt from morning chores. His face was calm as he watched the monkey with a curious but unreadable expression.

"I suppose I am," the monkey said shortly, his tail flicking.

The student studied him for a moment, then sat on a nearby rock. "You don't look like the others who come seeking the master."

The monkey let out a sharp scoff. "That's because I don't even know what I'm looking for."

The student smiled faintly. "I understand." His voice drifted off as he gazed toward the distant treetops.

The monkey glanced at him suspiciously. "And?"

The student hesitated. "Before I came here, I lived in a village by the river. My family was there, my friends—everything I had ever known. But somehow, I always felt like an outsider. Like I didn't quite belong, even among the people who raised me."

The monkey frowned. "What... you too?"

The student grinned slightly. "Yeah. I thought maybe coming here would change that. That I'd finally feel at home."

The monkey's eyes narrowed. "And do you?"

The student hesitated again. "Some days... Other days, I still feel like I'm looking for something I can't name."

The monkey's tail lashed sharply against the ground. "So what are you saying? That no matter where we go, we'll never belong anywhere?"

The student met his gaze with a quiet expression. "I don't know. But I do know that leaving one place doesn't always mean you've escaped what was inside you all along."

The monkey exhaled sharply, rubbing his temples. "Well, that's... not helpful."

The student simply smiled, as if he'd expected that answer.

After a long pause, the monkey pushed himself to his feet, brushing the dust from his fur. "I have to keep looking."

The student didn't try to stop him. He simply nodded.

With that, the monkey set off again, his frustration deepening.

He climbed the mountain for days, each step pulling him further from the jungle he had always known. His arms ached from scaling rocky ledges, his fingers scraped raw against jagged stone. The cold mountain air bit at his skin, so different from the thick, humid jungle.

Below him, the dense canopy had disappeared, replaced by an endless stretch of jagged peaks and eerie silence. His thoughts were his only company, looping in endless circles—dwelling on old grievances, moments of loneliness, the gnawing sense that something was missing.

And then, at last, he reached the summit.

There, at the edge of a vast ravine, sat the old master, legs crossed, eyes half-closed, as if listening to something only he could hear.

The monkey froze mid-step. His mouth went dry. *What? How did he get here?*

He hesitated, his pulse quickening. Then, cautiously, he sat beside the master, eyeing him sideways.

"Master," he said, his voice quieter than usual in the stillness. "Is it you?"

Silence.

The monkey shifted, his tail curling tightly around his feet. "Master, I..." He faltered, unsure if he should continue.

More silence.

The monkey's patience snapped. His fingers clenched in the dirt. "Master, I feel like I don't belong anywhere!" The words burst out before he could stop them. "In the jungle, I'm different from the other monkeys. When I travel, I am a stranger. Even now, sitting beside you, I feel... apart."

The master slowly opened his eyes and gazed out at the ravine before them. "What do you see?"

The monkey followed his gaze. A great chasm stretched between two cliffs, deep and endless. The sun cast long shadows into its depths, making it seem even more unreachable.

He hesitated. "I see..." His brow furrowed. "A vast space. A valley between two mountains."

The master gave a small nod. "Yes. And what else?"

The monkey looked again. The jagged cliffs framed the empty air between them. He studied the steep drops, the rugged edges of stone. "It's... uncrossable."

The master remained silent, waiting.

The monkey shifted uncomfortably. "One side is over there, the other side is here." He exhaled. "Separate."

The master tilted his head slightly. "And if you were a bird, flying above?"

The monkey blinked. He pictured himself soaring through the crisp air, his feet never touching the ground. The image flickered in his mind. "Then..." He frowned, something clicking into place. "Then there would be no divide. Just one mountain."

The master smiled. "Perspective shapes perception. The separation you see exists only from where you stand."

The monkey frowned, staring at the ravine. "But it's real. I can't cross it."

The master reached into his robe and pulled out a small wooden cup. He dipped it into a nearby stream and held it up, the water glistening in the light. "Is the water in this cup separate from the stream?"

The monkey tilted his head. "Well... yes. It's in the cup now."

The master poured the water back into the stream. Ripples spread outward, dissolving any trace of separation. "And now?"

The monkey watched with raised eyebrows. The water that had been in the cup was now indistinguishable from the rest.

"We create separation in our minds," the master continued. "We label things: me, you; here, there; past, future. But is a wave separate from the ocean? Or a leaf from the tree?"

The monkey scratched his chin. "But I *feel* separate. When others do not understand me. When I am alone."

The master picked up a pebble and rolled it between his fingers before tossing it into the ravine. They listened as it clattered down the rocky walls, the sound gradually fading into silence. "Does the stone leave the mountain?"

The monkey thought for a moment. His fingers absently traced patterns in the dirt. "No... It is still part of it, just in a different place."

The master placed a hand over his heart. "So too are we. The mind builds walls that do not exist. Whether you stand on one side of the mountain or the other, you are always part of something greater."

The monkey exhaled. He looked again at the ravine, turning the thought over in his mind. *It's not an impassable divide, but part of the whole landscape.*

He understood the words—but was it truly that simple? Could a thought alone dissolve something that had always felt so real?

The breeze stirred the dust at his feet. He inhaled deeply, feeling the mountain air fill his chest.

Strangely, he felt... a little less alone.

Pause & Reflect

Where in your life do you feel separate or disconnected from others? How might you experience change if you saw yourself as part of a greater whole?

Chapter 3
Returning to the Self

The wandering monkey had fallen asleep on the mountain, curled beneath a sheltering tree. When he opened his eyes, the sun was already high in the sky. He stretched his stiff limbs and blinked groggily.

The master was nowhere to be seen.

Had it been a dream?

He sat up slowly, his mind still tangled with the memory of the master's presence on the mountain. *How could the master have been there when he'd left him in the temple?*

With a sigh, he dusted himself off and made his way down the mountain. His mind churned.

By the time he arrived at the temple just before dusk, his fur was covered in dust, his muscles aching from the descent. But it was not just his body that felt weary—there was something deeper, a restlessness that no amount of walking could shake.

Along his journey, he had met many creatures, each with their own way of being. He had imitated the wise turtle's steady posture, the tiger's roaring confidence, even the crane's meditative stillness. Yet, with each new role, he felt no closer to understanding himself. Instead, he felt as though he was drifting further away, like a leaf caught in the wind, never quite landing anywhere.

As he entered the quiet courtyard at the temple, he found the old master tending to a small bonsai tree. The master's fingers moved with careful precision, shaping the tiny branches with delicate snips of his shears. Without looking up, he gestured for the monkey to sit.

The monkey's tail hovered in the air for a moment. He had taken all day to get back. How had the master arrived so quickly? He shook his head, deciding not to ask. Instead, he took a hesitant step forward and lowered himself onto the stone bench.

"Master," he began, rubbing the back of his neck, "I have studied many ways of being. I have learned to be quiet like the fox, strong like the ox, and patient like the river. But no matter what I do, I never feel whole. Who am I truly meant to be?"

The master set down his shears and regarded the monkey for a long moment. Then, he stood and motioned for the monkey to follow.

They walked in silence until they reached a stone basin filled with water. The surface reflected the vast sky above, streaked with the last golden light of day.

"Look into the water," the master said. "What do you see?"

The monkey peered into the still surface. "My reflection."

He frowned. *Hadn't the master already shown him this lesson before?*

The master picked up a smooth stone and tossed it into the basin. Ripples spread outward, distorting the image.

"And now?"

"My face is broken," the monkey muttered with impatience. "It is no longer clear."

Hardly a moment had passed before he exclaimed, "Yes, yes, I know—you already told me about..." He stopped himself, teeth clenching with mild irritation.

But the master remained silent, watching as the water slowly settled. Only when the last ripple faded did he speak.

"Each time you adopt another's way, you stir the surface of your being. You seek yourself in reflections that are not your own. That is why you never feel whole."

The monkey exhaled sharply, crossing his arms. "Then how do I know which reflection is the real me?"

The master smiled. "Tell me, who were you before you began trying to be someone else?"

The monkey opened his mouth to retort, then paused. His thoughts drifted beyond his recent travels, beyond the many creatures he had mimicked, back to when he had not questioned who he was. He remembered the thrill of leaping through the trees for the sheer joy of movement, the way he used to laugh when the wind playfully tousled his fur, the times he sat in stillness without wondering whether he was doing it *correctly*.

The master's voice was calm, steady. "The tree does not ask how to be a tree. The river does not seek to flow like the wind. They are as they are. The search for the self is only needed when we forget who we have always been."

The monkey looked again at the water. The surface was still now, clear and unbroken. His reflection stared back at him—not as something to be shaped or fixed, but as something that had always been enough.

The frustration that had gripped him only moments ago dissolved like mist in the morning sun. A slow smile spread across his face. For the first time in a long while, he did not feel the need to look away.

Pause & Reflect

In what ways have you tried to shape yourself into an identity that wasn't truly yours? What happens when you allow yourself to just be?

Chapter 4
The Quiet Magic of Trust

Over the next few days, the wandering monkey decided to explore the jungle near the temple. The air hummed with unfamiliar sounds and scents, different from the jungle he had once called home. Everything felt both new and strangely distant, as if he were seeing the world through a lens he had never used before.

He moved through the dense foliage, swinging and weaving effortlessly from tree to tree. Somewhere nearby, a troop of monkeys chattered, their calls bouncing between the towering trees like playful echoes.

Then, out of the blue, he found himself clinging to the edge of a tree branch, staring at the gap between where he was and where he needed to be.

It wasn't far. Just one leap, and he would reach the next branch. He had done this a thousand times before. But today, for some reason, he hesitated.

The wind whistled through the trees, rustling the leaves like whispers of unseen spirits. The scent of fresh moss rose from below, where the jungle floor stretched out in shadowy depths. His grip tightened on the bark beneath his fingers.

What if I miss? What if I slip?

His breath came quicker.

This isn't my jungle. It's a new jungle.

His muscles tensed, coiled like a spring, but his mind refused to release him. He had never been afraid of jumping before. Yet now, as he stood frozen on the branch, his thoughts were louder than his instincts.

A familiar voice drifted up from below.

"Ah, little one," the old master called, standing beside the roots of the towering tree. "Why do you stand still when you wish to move?"

The monkey didn't loosen his grip. "Master!"

He didn't know whether he was more relieved or embarrassed. "Master... what if I fall?"

The master smiled, his gaze warm with knowing. "And what if you don't?"

The monkey's heart pounded. "I... I don't know."

The master pointed toward the river winding through the jungle in the distance. "Tell me, does the river pause before it meets the waterfall?"

The monkey blinked, glancing at the glistening ribbon of water that rushed ever forward, spilling over jagged rocks into the unknown below.

"No," he muttered. "It just... flows."

The master nodded. "And the birds—do they question the air before they spread their wings?"

The monkey turned his head. A pair of sparrows flitted between the trees, darting and gliding through the wind with effortless grace. They never hesitated. Never doubted.

"No," he admitted. "They just trust."

The master chuckled. "Yes. They trust. Not because they know what will happen, but because they know themselves."

The monkey held his breath. His fingers dug into the bark as he stared at the gap in front of him.

His fear was not real—it was a shadow, a story his mind was telling him. His body already knew what to do. It had always known.

He inhaled deeply, letting the crisp mountain air fill his lungs. The wind brushed against his fur, urging him forward, reminding him of the thousands of leaps before this one.

And then, before he could think any longer, he jumped.

For a heartbeat, there was nothing but air beneath him. The world slowed, his breath caught—

And then, his hands found the next branch. His feet steadied. The rough bark pressed firm beneath his fingers.

He had done it.

The master nodded approvingly. "You see, little one? Magic is not in certainty. Magic is in trusting yourself anyway."

The monkey let out a breath of relief, feeling his heart slow. He looked back at the branch where he had stood frozen in doubt and then at the empty space he had feared—and smiled.

Perhaps trust wasn't about knowing the outcome.

Perhaps it was about moving forward, even when you don't.

Pause & Reflect

Where in your life do you feel drawn to take a leap but find yourself hesitating? What thoughts or emotions arise when you imagine trusting the path ahead?

Chapter 5
The Stories We Weave

The wandering monkey stormed into the temple courtyard just as the evening lanterns were being lit. Their warm glow flickered against the ancient stone walls, casting long shadows across the courtyard. A gentle breeze carried the scent of sweet osmanthus through the air, and the distant sound of laughter from the students echoed softly between the columns.

But the monkey did not notice any of it. His mood was the very opposite of the tranquil space he'd just entered.

How dare they?

His breath came quick, his chest tight. It wasn't the first time this had happened.

He'd been exploring a nearby village when a group of humans spotted him. Some had laughed, pointing at him as if he were nothing more than a foolish creature. Others had spoken in hushed whispers, shaking their heads as he passed. And one—a man with a heavy voice—had even scoffed, "Look at the little monkey. He thinks he's one of us."

The words clung to his mind like bristles caught in his fur, refusing to be shaken loose. His hands clenched into fists.

Why do they see me this way?

He replayed the scene again and again—the sneers, the dismissive looks, the way the man's voice had curled with amusement. The thoughts looped in his mind, each repetition adding fuel to his anger.

The old master sat beside the firepit in the courtyard, serenely watching the flickering flames. His presence was steady, unshaken, as if he had been waiting for the monkey to arrive.

The monkey threw himself down beside the master with a huff, arms crossed tightly over his chest. The master glanced at him and murmured. "Ah. The storm has arrived."

The monkey scowled. "People judge me, Master. They assume they know me, but they don't. They make up stories about who I am. And no matter what I do, I can't change it."

The master picked up a dry twig from the ground and held it over the fire. The flames caught instantly, curling black along the edges.

"And what story do you tell yourself about them?" the master asked.

The monkey squinted at the master. "What do you mean?"

The master gently blew on the burning twig. The ember flared, then died, leaving behind only fragile charcoal. He crumbled it between his fingers, the dust scattering into the wind.

"You see their words," the master said, "and like this twig, you let them catch fire in your mind. You watch them burn, and the flames grow, until you are certain they are true."

The monkey frowned, watching the specks of ash drift into the night air.

"But was the twig ever truly fire?" the master continued. "Or was it only something that burned because it was fed?"

The monkey wavered. "It was just a twig. It only became fire when you set it alight."

The master smiled. "And so it is with stories. You heard laughter, and you told yourself a story—that they see you as a fool. You heard whispers, and you told yourself another story—that you are unworthy. But were those words truly flames? Or did you let them burn inside you?"

The monkey's tail flicked sharply. "But what if it's true?"

The master chuckled, his voice low and knowing. "And what if it is not? Perhaps they were laughing at something else. Perhaps the whispers were about their own troubles. And even if their judgments were real, do their stories shape who you are? Or do you?"

The monkey watched as the last of the ash faded into the breeze. He thought of how quickly he had accepted the villagers' laughter as proof of his foolishness. How easily he had taken their words and fed them until they burned.

The master spoke again, his voice gentle. "You will always hear stories, little one—some told by others, some whispered by your own mind. But not all stories are true. And not all are yours to carry."

The monkey sat still. For the first time, he wondered how many stories he had believed that were never real at all.

He took a deep breath, letting the cool night air fill his lungs.

Perhaps it was time to tell himself a different story.

A few days passed. The monkey carried the master's words with him, turning them over in his mind. He noticed how often his thoughts spun stories—how quickly his mind filled in the gaps with assumptions.

But knowing this did not make it easy to stop.

One evening, as the sun dipped behind the mountains, he sat in the temple courtyard, watching the students finish their evening tasks. One of them—an older student he had seen many times but never spoken to—settled onto the stone steps beside him.

"You look deep in thought," the student said, stretching out his legs.

The monkey sighed. "I'm trying not to believe every story my mind tells me."

The student chuckled. "A difficult task."

They sat in companionable silence for a moment before the student spoke again. "I used to do the same thing, you know—believe the wrong stories."

The monkey glanced at him, intrigued. "What do you mean?"

The student rubbed a hand over his knee, as if remembering something distant. "There was once a man in my village I despised. He never spoke to me, never even looked my way. I convinced myself he thought he was above me, that he saw me as small and insignificant. I carried that belief for years, letting it fester into anger. Whenever I saw him, my stomach twisted with resentment."

The monkey leaned forward, eager to know more.

The student let out a small laugh. "One day, I finally spoke to him, and do you know what he said?"

The monkey shook his head.

"He told me he had always assumed *I* thought *he* was beneath me. That I was the one who had no interest in talking."

The monkey blinked. "You both believed the same story—about each other?"

The student nodded. "And for years, we both suffered for it."

The monkey was quiet.

How many times had he done the same? Taken a glance, a whisper, a laugh—and spun it into a story that hurt him? How often had he assumed the worst and made himself suffer for it?

A breeze stirred the lanterns above them, their light flickering gently. The monkey stared at the golden glow, letting the realization settle.

At last, he spoke. "So how do you stop believing the wrong stories?"

The student smiled. "You ask yourself one question."

The monkey looked puzzled. "What question?"

The student met his gaze. "What else could be true?"

The monkey let the words sink in.

He thought of the villagers' laughter, the whispers, the man who had scoffed. He had assumed they mocked him. *But what else could be true? Maybe they had been amused by something else. Maybe the whispers had nothing to do with him. Maybe the man's words had come from his own insecurities, not from truth.*

Maybe, just maybe, the stories he had told himself were never real at all.

A slow smile tugged at his lips.

He still had much to learn. But tonight, he would begin by asking himself a different question.

What else could be true?

Above them, the lanterns swayed in the wind, their glow steady against the night.

And in his mind, the ember of a new story flickered to life.

Pause & Reflect

What stories have you been telling yourself about who you are or how the world sees you? Are they true, or are they just reflections of old fears? What else could be true?

Chapter 6
Everything Echoes

Several days later, the wandering monkey sat with the temple students. For the first time in a long while, he felt lighter—freer than he had in years. Though the echoes of the past still lingered in the corners of his mind, this evening, he was in high spirits.

He had been telling the temple students all about his travels—his daring adventures, the strange creatures he had encountered, the lessons he had learned. The students hung on every word, their eyes wide with awe.

A student turned to him and smiled. "You've seen so much of the world, had so many amazing experiences."

Warmth bloomed in his chest.

As the sun dipped below the horizon, he left them in the courtyard, smiling to himself as the sound of their chatter faded in the distance. But just as he stepped onto the path leading back to his quarters, the same old memory surfaced—one he had tried to forget.

A particular village. A particular crowd. The way they had gawked at him, laughed, even thrown stones to chase him away.

His mood darkened instantly, his high spirits vanishing into thin air.

No. I know better now. This is just another story. I'm supposed to be telling myself a different story.

The lesson with the master sprang to mind but it eluded him.

Every laugh, every sneer, every dismissive glance played in his head like a loop he could not escape. By the time he reached the temple, he felt like a storm cloud, ready to burst.

The old master was sweeping leaves from the stone path, his movements slow and steady, unbothered by the world beyond the temple walls. He did not look up as the monkey stormed forward, pacing in tight circles.

"Master," the monkey huffed, his tail thrashing, "why are people so unkind? When I was passing through the village, the people whispered, pointed, laughed. Some even threw stones. Why do they judge without knowing? I wasn't even speaking to them! I was only curious, only watching, but they looked at me like I didn't belong."

His voice grew sharper, his breath unsteady. "I know I talked about this before, but I did nothing to them. I should have said something back. I should have made them see that I was more than just a monkey!"

But even as he spoke, he knew the words felt worn—like a song he didn't even like but kept playing over and over.

The master leaned against his broom, observing him with calm, patient eyes. Without a word, he gestured for the monkey to follow.

They walked through the temple's quiet corridors, the air cool and filled with the faint scent of sandalwood. Instead of stopping inside, the master led him beyond the temple walls, up a narrow path that climbed to the mountain's peak.

The wind whispered through the craggy stones, carrying with it the distant cries of birds.

At the edge of the cliff, the master turned and gestured toward the vast emptiness before them.

"Shout your anger into the valley."

The monkey hesitated, but the master gave him an expectant nod. He took a deep breath and roared, "You are all fools!" His voice thundered through the mountains, vanishing for a moment into the void.

Then, it came back.

"You are all fools!"

The words were flung back at him as if spat by the very air itself.

The monkey flinched. A rush of heat crawled up his neck. His ears burned. He hadn't expected to hear his own rage thrown back at him so clearly.

His fingers clenched into fists as he shouted again, louder this time—

"You don't understand me!"

And again, the mountains answered.

"You don't understand me!"

The monkey's stomach tightened. His breath caught in his throat. With each echo, his own voice sounded more bitter, more helpless.

His own anger—flung back at him, again and again.

The master smiled faintly. "Now, speak kindness."

The monkey hesitated again but obeyed. This time, his voice was softer. "May you all find peace."

For a breath, there was silence. Then, carried on the wind, came the reply: "May you all find peace."

The monkey's ears twitched. The valley had returned his words just as they were given.

The master sat on a smooth stone, hands resting in his lap. "The world is an echo, little one. If you send anger into it, anger returns. If you send kindness, kindness finds its way back."

The monkey looked down at his hands, his feelings still tangled. "But... the villagers insulted me first." The memory still burned. He could feel the sting—not just of their mockery, but at the injustice of it.

The master smiled. "Did they? Or did you enter their village with suspicion, already expecting to be mocked? Tell me, little one, if you had walked in with warmth, what might have been echoed back?"

The monkey thought of the villagers, the laughter, the stares.

Had he met them with a closed heart? Had he already decided they would see him as a fool before they had a chance to do otherwise?

Then...

Would it mean their words didn't matter? But they did.

Would it mean their cruelty was acceptable? But it wasn't.

Would it mean he had lost?

The wind stirred around them, cool and cleansing. The monkey took a deep breath.

"I see," he murmured. "The world speaks back what we send into it."

The master smiled. "Not always immediately. But in time, yes. And when you change the call, the echo changes, too."

The monkey sat there a little longer, listening to the wind, wondering how many times he had shouted anger into the world and mistaken its echo for truth.

Pause & Reflect

Are there burdens from the past that still weigh on you? How do they feel when you bring them to mind? What might it be like to imagine releasing them, even for a moment?

Chapter 7
The Joy of No Agenda

The wandering monkey's mind was brimming with urgency. He had woken that morning with the nagging feeling that something was missing, though he couldn't quite place what. His thoughts buzzed and questions still weighed heavily upon him. One question burned the most. Perhaps today, he would finally gain the wisdom he sought.

He marched through the temple grounds until he found the old master, seated beneath a large cherry blossom tree, his gaze following the delicate petals as they drifted lazily in the breeze.

The monkey cleared his throat, eager to begin. This was important.

"Master," he said, his voice filled with intent, "today, I wish to learn something new."

The master nodded but said nothing. He continued watching the blossoms, his face serene, as if he had all the time in the world.

The monkey shifted impatiently. "Perhaps you can give me a lesson on patience?"

Still, the master remained silent.

The monkey's tail swished.

"Or wisdom?" the monkey suggested, a hint of irritation creeping into his tone.

Nothing.

The monkey let out an exasperated sigh, his shoulders slumping dramatically. "Master, are we not going to do something useful?"

At last, the master turned to him and smiled. "We *are* doing something."

The monkey frowned deeply. "What are we doing?"

The master gestured toward the tree. "We are watching the petals fall."

The monkey looked bewildered as he followed the master's gaze. The pink petals twirled in the air, some landing gently on the grass, others caught in unseen currents, floating further than the eye could follow.

He looked from the master to the tree, then back again, waiting.

Nothing happened.

His impatience boiled over.

"That is not learning! That is just sitting and waiting for something to happen," he protested, throwing his arms in the air for emphasis.

The master's eyes crinkled in amusement. "Tell me, little one, what is the tree's goal in letting go of its blossoms?"

The monkey scratched his head, scoffing at the same time. "It has no goal. The petals simply fall."

The master nodded. "And yet, see how they dance on the wind, how they create beauty without trying. The tree does not chase the wind. It does not demand the petals fall in a certain way. It simply allows."

The monkey folded his arms, his frustration bubbling over. "But that is different! I am not a tree. I must do something. I must seek, strive, achieve! If I do nothing, how will I ever grow?"

He couldn't contain his impatience—the very opposite of his desire to learn it.

Still, the master said nothing, only watching the petals drift and sway.

The monkey huffed loudly, then planted himself firmly on the ground, determined to at least pretend to be patient.

For a moment, he watched the petals.

And then—

A petal floated toward him.

Suddenly this became imperative—if he was going to do nothing, then he was at least going to do nothing well.

He stuck out his hand, trying to catch the petal.

It danced just out of reach.

His tail twitched.

A new mission was born.

Catch the petal.

He shifted his stance, arms raised, watching the petals intensely. He jumped. He lunged. He waved his arms wildly, willing the petals to fall into his grasp.

But every time, his hand closed around nothing but air.

The master let out a soft sigh and reached up, effortlessly plucking a petal from the air. He held it between his fingers, letting the monkey observe it closely. "Tell me, if this petal were to resist the wind, what would happen?"

The monkey narrowed his eyes. "That's foolish. A petal can't resist the wind."

The master tilted his head. "And yet, you resist life in the same way."

The monkey held his breath. He started to argue but found no words. He stared at the petal, then at the countless others floating freely.

He had spent his life grasping, reaching, always demanding answers. But now, watching the effortless dance of the petals, he felt something move within him—something unsettling yet oddly comforting.

The master continued, "You came here today wanting something to happen. Wanting knowledge. Wanting progress. But wisdom does not always arrive when summoned. Sometimes, it comes when you stop chasing it."

The monkey exhaled, his shoulders loosening slightly. Yet, a quiet voice in the back of his mind resisted. *If I stop seeking, what if I never find? What if I become lost?*

Still, he hesitated, caught between his old habit of striving and the strange stillness of the moment.

The master smiled knowingly. "Just as the wind carries the petal, life carries you. But only if you let it."

The monkey sat beside the master, watching the petals fall. He tried—tried—to release the weight of expectation, to allow himself to be carried like the petal in the wind.

But deep inside, he wasn't sure if he was ready to let go—or if he even knew how.

Pause & Reflect

Where in your life do you feel caught in striving or chasing? What might it be like to loosen your grip and allow things to unfold in their own time?

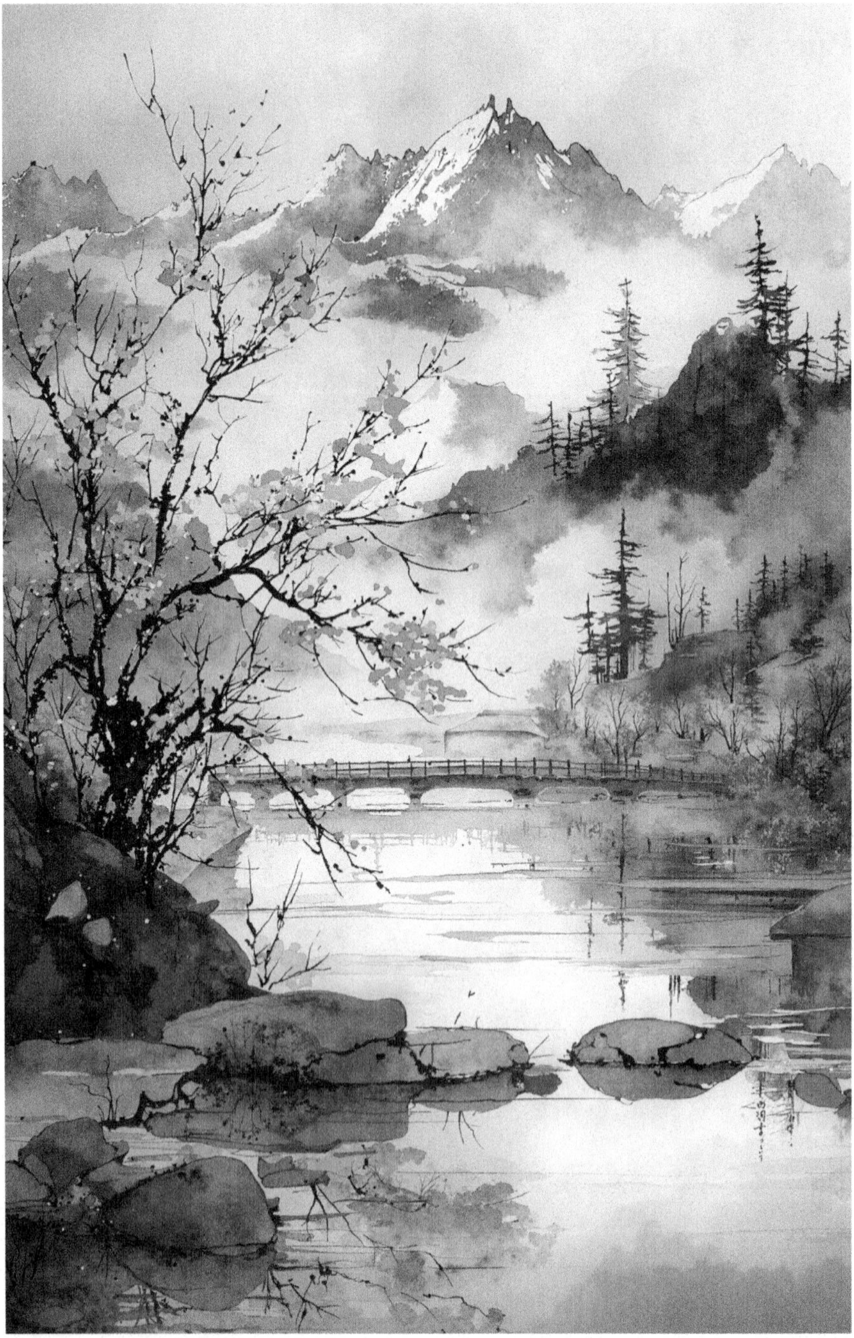

Chapter 8
Relax Into Receiving

The wandering monkey was exhausted. His mind churned with restless thoughts, chasing wisdom, searching for answers, grasping for something—anything—that would bring him peace. But the more he searched, the more elusive peace became.

And though the master's lesson beneath the cherry blossom tree was still fresh in his mind, the truth had not yet taken root in him. He had been told to release his agenda, to trust the flow of life, but how could he? Surely, without an agenda, nothing could be gained.

As the monkey made his way toward the temple, still wrestling with doubt, he noticed a young temple student walking the same path. The student's face was tense, his brows furrowed in thought.

The monkey had seen him before, but they had never spoken. Now, something about the student's expression mirrored his own frustration.

The student sighed and muttered to himself.

"What's troubling you?" the monkey asked, falling into step beside him.

The student hesitated, then gave him a tired smile. "I expect too much," he admitted. "I work hard, I follow the teachings, I try to do everything right… and yet, I still feel restless. I thought that if I practiced enough, I would find peace. But it never lasts."

The monkey raised an eyebrow. "You think peace should come just because you've worked for it?"

The student snorted. "Shouldn't it?"

The monkey let out a breath. "I've been asking myself the same thing."

They walked in silence for a moment before the student spoke again.

"I keep waiting for things to happen the way I imagine them. I think, 'Once I get this, I'll feel at peace,' or, 'Once I understand that, I'll finally be free.' But no matter what I reach, there is always something else just beyond it."

The monkey stopped walking. He turned to look at the student, realization dawning. "That's exactly what I do."

The student let out a soft laugh. "Seems we're chasing the same thing."

The monkey nodded. He had expected to feel alone in this struggle. But now, standing beside the student, he saw that he was not the only one caught in this endless cycle of expectation.

They exchanged a glance, then, without another word, continued toward the master together.

When they reached the temple, they found the old master sitting by a gentle stream, his feet dipped into the cool water. The master looked up and smiled. "Come, sit, both of you. Tell me what weighs on you."

The student and the monkey exchanged a look. Then, together, they sat by the water.

"I try so hard," the monkey admitted. "I seek knowledge, I meditate, I practice discipline. But the peace I search for never stays. The more I chase it, the further it seems to run."

The student nodded. "And I struggle to let go of expectations. I always think I'm supposed to be further along than I am."

The master smiled. "Ah. Then I have something to show you both."

He reached into the water with an open hand. The current flowed freely through his fingers, swirling around his palm.

"Now, try to take some water for yourselves," he instructed.

The monkey and the student plunged their hands into the stream, squeezing tightly to grab as much water as they could. But when they lifted their hands, the water had slipped through their fingers, leaving only a few droplets.

The student scowled, flicking his fingers. "It's impossible to hold onto it."

The monkey huffed, looking up at the master. "The tighter I hold, the less I have."

The master chuckled, watching them with knowing eyes. "Now, try again. But this time, relax your hands."

They hesitated. Then slowly, they lowered their hands gently into the stream, keeping them open without grasping or forcing. The water pooled in their open palms, resting there lightly, undisturbed.

Both the monkey and student stared wide-eyed at the water in their palms, astonished at how it stayed without effort.

"Peace is like water," the master continued. "If you chase it, it will slip through your grasp. If you hold on too tightly, it will disappear. But if you relax and allow, it will come to you naturally."

The student glanced at the master. "So, if I stop expecting things to be a certain way... life will flow?"

The master leaned back, resting his hands behind his head. "Not just life. Everything."

The monkey exhaled, and still, something within him resisted. *But if I stop striving, how will I know I am making progress?* The thought clung to him, just as his hands had clung to the water.

Sensing their hesitation, the master asked, "Tell me, did either of you do anything special to deserve the air you breathe?"

The monkey blinked. "No."

"It's just... there," frowned the student.

"Yet it is given freely," the master said. "So too is peace, so too is the unfolding of life."

The monkey and the student exchanged glances.

They had both invested tremendous effort into reaching, grasping, expecting—never realizing that what they sought had always been there, waiting to be received.

The student let out a breath, shoulders relaxing. The monkey flexed his fingers, watching as the last drops of water slid from his palm.

They sat in silence, watching the stream flow on, the lesson sinking in—not through effort, not through force, but through gentle acceptance.

For the first time since they could remember, they both simply relaxed and allowed themselves to be.

Pause & Reflect

Think of a time when something you desired came effortlessly, without struggle. How can you become more open to receiving rather than striving?

Something for You – Free Zen-Inspired Gifts

The wisdom in *The Monkey and the Way of Zen* isn't just to be read—it's to be experienced. To support your journey beyond these pages, I've prepared a collection of gentle offerings for you to receive:

- **The Monkey's Zen Companion** – A quick guide to the core Zen teaching behind each story.
- **The Dance of Coming Home** – An exclusive short story with one final conversation between the monkey and the master.
- **The Art of Gentle Presence** – Five simple, 2-minute practices to quiet overthinking and find peace.
- **The Way of the Quiet Mind** – A meditation guide with recorded practices to embody the book's lessons.
- **Reflections from the Monkey's Journey** – 6 mobile phone wallpapers featuring inspiring quotes from the stories.

These gifts are yours. May they remind you of the stillness beneath the noise, the space between the stories, and the infinite sky within.

Download your free gifts here:
https://bonuses.serenachoo.com/monkey-zen-unlock-your-bonuses/ or scan the QR code.

40 THE MONKEY AND THE WAY OF ZEN

Chapter 9
The Body's Quiet Wisdom

The wandering monkey had discovered a new section of the jungle, and to him, that was better than finding a chest full of golden bananas.

All day, he swung from vines, leapt between trees, and raced along narrow branches like a gust of wind. He hurled himself onto piles of soft moss, stumbled upon hidden waterfalls, startled a family of parrots, and even found a particularly large leaf that made an excellent hat.

For hours, he roamed, playing, laughing, and testing his limits.

But as the sun dipped lower in the sky, he realized something.

He had no idea where he was.

Pausing on a thick branch, he scratched his head.

With a sigh, the monkey picked a random direction and charged ahead, determined to find his way home.

And that was where things started to go wrong.

The dense jungle thinned into steep, rocky terrain. The ground became uneven, sharp edges jutting out like jagged teeth. The playful energy that had fueled him all morning was quickly replaced by aching limbs and a grumbling stomach.

Still, he pressed on. He gritted his teeth and marched onward, ignoring the dull throb in his legs. His mind screamed at him to keep going, to fight through the discomfort, to not give in. But now, his feet hurt, and every muscle protested with fatigue.

Then his foot slipped on loose gravel. With a startled yelp, he tumbled down the rocky incline, bouncing like a dropped coconut before coming to an undignified stop at the bottom.

He winced, dragging himself to his feet. His body ached, his stomach growled, and his once-flawless leaf hat was gone.

By the time he reached the temple, his body was running on nothing but stubbornness.

The old master sat beneath a mango tree, peeling fruit with a small knife. He looked up as the monkey approached, his sharp eyes taking in the monkey's sluggish steps, his drooping ears, his patchy and uneven fur.

"Where have you come from, little one?" the master asked.

The monkey flopped onto the ground, limbs spread dramatically.

"I discovered a new part of the jungle! It was amazing! I swung, I climbed…" Then he scowled. "I got lost!" He relayed his arduous return journey, his voice now tinged with annoyance.

"I don't get it, Master. I listen to wise words, I practice discipline, and I train my mind. But my body is a burden! It gets tired, it gets hungry, it slows me down."

The master chuckled and handed the monkey a slice of mango.

"Eat," he said simply.

The monkey hesitated for half a second before grabbing the fruit and stuffing it into his mouth. The sweetness burst on his tongue, and a low sigh of relief escaped him. Only then did he realize how hungry he had been.

The master watched him. "Did your mind tell you to eat, or did your body?"

The monkey licked juice from his fingers. "My body… I suppose."

The master nodded. "Your body speaks to you, but you do not always listen."

The monkey tilted his head, chewing over the words. "But I listen to my mind. Isn't that the path to wisdom?"

The master smiled. "Your mind is full of stories. But your body knows truth."

He picked up a fallen mango from the ground and held it out.

"Tell me, is this fruit good to eat?"

The monkey sniffed it and immediately gagged. "No, it's rotten!"

"How did you know?"

The monkey blinked. "I just... felt it."

The master tossed the mango aside.

"Your body knew without needing to think. Just as it knows when to eat, when to rest, when to move. Yet so often, we silence its wisdom with the noise of our minds."

The monkey thought of his aching feet, his exhaustion, the hunger he had ignored for hours. He had pushed himself forward, demanding more, ignoring every signal his body had sent him.

"So... my body was never a burden," he murmured. "It was trying to help me?"

The master smiled. "It always has been."

The monkey stared at his tired hands, feeling a quiet gratitude. He had always been fighting his body, pushing it, treating it as an obstacle.

But now, he saw it differently.

Not as a weight to carry—but as a wise companion on his journey.

With a newfound appreciation, he took another bite of mango, savoring it fully.

For once, he truly listened to more than just his mind.

Pause & Reflect

Do you listen to your body's messages, or do you push through discomfort? What might change if you treated your body as a wise messenger rather than something to control?

Chapter 10
Life Unfolding for You

The wandering monkey was having a bad day. After savoring the delicious mango the master had given him the day before, he had spent all this morning searching for ripe mangoes, only to find the trees bare.

Then, as he climbed a rocky path toward the temple, he slipped, tumbling down the hillside, leaving scratches on his arms and dust in his fur. His knees grazed, his pride was wounded, and his stomach growled in protest.

Even before he reached the temple, he could hear the laughter of the temple students. They were clearly taking a break from their studies, enjoying the afternoon. It annoyed him even more that the students seemed to be having a good time.

The old master seated by the fire, eyed him knowingly. "Ah, little one. You look like a storm rolling in."

The monkey threw up his hands. "Master, I tried to find mangoes, but there were none. Then I fell on the rocky path and look at my arms! Life keeps getting in my way!"

The master nodded thoughtfully, then reached into a basket beside him and pulled out a bundle of herbs. "Come, help me prepare tea."

Still fuming, the monkey plopped down beside him. The master handed him a handful of leaves. "Crush these," he instructed.

The monkey frowned but did as he was told, grinding the leaves between his fingers. Their scent filled the air, sharp and fresh.

The master nodded. "Good. Now, taste one."

The monkey hesitated, then popped a leaf into his mouth. Instantly, he gagged. "Ugh! It's bitter!"

The master chuckled and dropped the rest into the steaming water. He stirred in silence, allowing the tea to brew. After a few moments, he poured two cups and handed one to the monkey.

"Drink," he said.

The monkey reluctantly took a sip. Then his eyes widened, eyebrows lifting in surprise. The tea was smooth, warm—soothing. "This is... good!"

The master smiled. "The same leaves that were bitter on their own have created something nourishing. The bitterness was not the end of their story—it was part of their transformation."

The monkey lowered his cup, deep in thought. His mind pushed back. *But what if life really is against me? What if I am meant to struggle?*

As if he could read the monkey's mind, the master continued, "You think life is working against you because you taste its bitterness before it is finished brewing. You search for mangoes and find none—perhaps because a storm will come tomorrow and ruin the fruit, and life is saving you the trouble of wasted effort. You fall on the path—perhaps because had you continued, a greater danger lay ahead."

The monkey's ears twitched. He wanted to believe the master, but skepticism clung to him like dried mud. "But... what if life isn't guiding me?" he murmured, "What if things just go wrong?"

The master tilted his head. "And what if things are going right in ways you do not yet understand?"

The monkey thought of all the times he had cursed his misfortunes, never considering that they might be leading him somewhere better.

But doubt still lingered. He wanted to trust that life was guiding him, but was it just telling himself a story to make himself feel better?

He sighed, staring down into his cup.

Perhaps life was not against him. Perhaps it had been offering him tea this whole time. And yet... what if bitterness was all there was? What if he let go of his fight, only to find himself lost? The thought unsettled him. The tea was warm, but his fingers still curled around the cup—uncertain, resisting.

He wasn't sure he was ready to loosen his grip just yet.

Pause & Reflect

Can you recall a time when something that seemed like a setback actually led to something better? How would your life feel different if you trusted that life is always working in your favor even before it makes sense?

Chapter 11
The Art of Active Waiting

The wandering monkey had been given just one task—he had been sent by the master to meet a visitor who would arrive "by midday."

While waiting, the monkey spent the morning moving from one thing to another, his energy restless and impatient. He collected fruit from the trees, arranged small stones into patterns, and even attempted to meditate—though his thoughts jumped as wildly as his feet often did.

He sighed and stretched dramatically, sprawling across the steps. He paced the courtyard twice, plucked three figs from a nearby tree, balanced on one foot just to see if it would make time move faster—and stacked small pebbles into a precarious tower, only to knock them over again.

And now, there was nothing left to do.

He sat on the temple steps, his tail thumping on the ground, his fingers drumming against the stone. The midday sun cast golden light over the courtyard, and in the distance, temple students moved about their tasks—sweeping leaves, tending to the garden, practicing slow, deliberate movements in their martial arts training.

And that was the problem.

He had no task, no purpose for the moment. Midday had come and gone, and there was no visitor in sight.

His mind itched with irritation. *What a waste of time. I could be doing something useful!*

Just then, the old master appeared from one of the temple halls, moving with his usual slow grace. He looked down at the monkey and smiled.

"Ah, little one," the master said, settling beside him on the steps. "You seem to be in deep conversation with yourself."

The monkey heaved an exaggerated sigh for effect, and flopped backward, staring at the sky. "I've been sitting here forever, waiting for this visitor to arrive, but nothing is happening! What's the point?"

The master picked up a single leaf that had fallen onto the steps. He turned it over in his fingers, examining its delicate veins. "Tell me, little one," he said, "what happens between the time a seed is planted and when it grows?"

The monkey sat up, intrigued. "Nothing."

The master raised an eyebrow. "Nothing?"

"Well… I mean, I can't see anything happening. But I suppose it's growing under the soil."

The master smiled. "Ah. So, is that nothing?"

The monkey shifted uncomfortably. "I guess not."

The master gestured to the sky. "And when the sun begins to set, does night come all at once?"

The monkey shook his head. "No… it happens gradually."

The master nodded. "You see, little one, the world moves in its own time. But because you do not see the movement, you assume there is none. You call waiting 'wasted time,' when in truth, it is the space where things quietly unfold."

The monkey frowned, staring at the now empty courtyard. His restlessness still lingered, but something about the master's words moved him.

He had always thought of waiting as an inconvenience, a dull pause between the interesting parts of life. Something to endure until the real thing—the thing that mattered—finally arrived.

The master continued, "The river does not rush to meet the sea. The fruit does not demand to ripen. The clouds do not hurry across the sky. Yet all things arrive, exactly when they are meant."

The monkey exhaled, rolling onto his back to stare up at the sky—again. But this time, he watched the lazy drift of a single cloud and felt the warm stone beneath him, its heat pressing into his back like a gentle hand.

For the first time since sitting down, he noticed the richness of the moment—not what was missing, but what was already there.

A breeze drifted through the courtyard, carrying the scent of freshly tilled earth from the temple garden. The rustling of leaves whispered a gentle rhythm.

He tapped his tail against the step, listening to the soft thudding sound. Had that sound been there all along? Had the world always been moving, even when he thought it was still?

Perhaps waiting was not empty after all.

The master smiled, as if sensing the shift. "Waiting is not emptiness, little one. It is a space—rich with possibility, with unseen movement, with life quietly arranging itself. Those who resist it feel only restlessness. Those who welcome it find peace in the unfolding."

Just then, a figure appeared in the distance, walking up the temple steps.

The visitor had arrived.

The monkey laughed out loud, a glint in his eye. *Of course. Just when I stop waiting, they show up.*

For the first time, he wondered if he had ever truly been waiting at all.

Pause & Reflect

How do you typically feel about waiting? What would change if you trusted that even in stillness, life is moving beneath the surface?

Chapter 12
The Spiral Path of Growth

The wandering monkey sat on a ledge high above the valley. Below him, the jungle stretched out in every direction, winding rivers cutting through the dense green like veins.

The old master sat beside him, silent as the wind. They had remained this way all morning. The monkey used to struggle with stillness, but today, he simply sat—with only the flicking of his tail giving away the fact that his mind was anything but quiet.

Finally, he spoke.

"Master," the monkey said, his voice quiet, "I'm confused. I have climbed this mountain before. I have sat here before. I thought I had learned the lessons of patience, trust, and surrender. But here I am again, with a mind crowded with familiar thoughts, familiar questions, old doubts." He shook his head, absently rolling a small stone between his fingers. "Have I really changed at all?"

The master gazed at the horizon, his expression unreadable. Then, without a word, he stood and began walking down the mountainside.

What? A silent lesson?

The monkey watched him for a moment, then followed.

The path twisted and turned, winding past familiar landmarks—the ancient banyan tree with its thick, gnarled roots, the rocky outcrop shaped like a lion's head, the bubbling stream that hummed with frogs.

He had walked this way many times before, and yet…

Something felt different.

He glanced at the path beneath his feet—at the same worn stones and twisting roots he had struggled with on his first climb.

That first ever journey up the mountain was still vivid in his memory.

He had been out of breath, his legs aching with every step. He had been irritated by the steep incline, annoyed at how long it took. He had grumbled about the tangled roots, cursed at the loose stones, and barely noticed the beauty around him.

His only thought back then had been: *When will I reach the top?*

Now… his legs still worked hard, but the struggle no longer felt unbearable. The roots were still there, the stones just as uneven—but he didn't trip over them as often. The jungle did not feel like an obstacle anymore.

Had the mountain changed?

Or had he?

They reached a clearing where wildflowers bloomed in every direction. The master stopped, gesturing around them.

"Tell me," the master said, "when you first walked this path, did you notice the flowers?"

The monkey blinked, looking around. The vibrant colors swayed gently in the breeze, petals open to the sun. Had they been here before?

"No... I suppose I didn't."

The master gestured toward the stream. "Did you hear the song of the frogs?"

The monkey's ears twitched as he listened. The croaking melody echoed through the clearing, rhythmic and soothing.

He smiled slightly. "I must have been too busy thinking."

The master nodded. "You see, you have walked this path before, but you are not the same monkey who walked it the first time."

As the monkey pondered the master's words, a memory surfaced.

A few days ago, a temple student had come to him, nervous about an upcoming lesson.

"I always get anxious," the student had admitted. "I feel like I never improve."

The monkey had reassured him, not thinking much of it.

But now, he realized...

He had once felt the exact same way. And somewhere along the way, he had become someone who didn't panic over every lesson. Who didn't constantly overthink every word the master spoke. Who could sit beside a student and sometimes offer reassurance instead of searching for it himself.

He *had* changed.

The master bent down and traced a spiral in the dirt.

"Growth is not a straight line, little one. It is a spiral. You may feel as if you are returning to the same place, but each time, you arrive with a deeper understanding."

The monkey followed the spiral's curves with his eyes.

So even if I feel like I am in the same place, I am actually further along?

He exhaled slowly, letting the idea settle.

The master continued. "The movement itself is growth. Each loop brings new awareness, even if challenges look familiar and your thoughts seem the same."

The master smiled, then turned, continuing up the mountain. The monkey followed, but this time, he walked slower, feeling the warmth of the earth beneath his feet, the rhythm of the wind in the trees, the scent of wild mint drifting through the air.

He was still learning, still growing.

But... he was further along than he thought.

Pause & Reflect

Have you ever felt like you were struggling with the same challenges over and over? Looking deeper, how have you actually grown each time you've faced a familiar challenge?

56 THE MONKEY AND THE WAY OF ZEN

Chapter 13
Responding, Not Reacting

The wandering monkey had been in deep reflection the last few days. He had learned much from the master, and many things that once annoyed him—the heat of the sun, the uneven path, the chatter of the birds—no longer bothered him in the same way. But one thing still infuriated him—his own inability to remain calm when things didn't go his way.

No matter how much he tried to remain peaceful, something always set him off. If someone spoke to him sharply, he snapped back. If an obstacle appeared in his path, frustration flared. If something didn't go as planned, his emotions would explode before he could even think.

And afterward? It always left him feeling worse.

As he wandered the temple grounds, his tail flicking irritably, he spotted a group of students sweeping the courtyard. Just then, one of the younger students accidentally bumped into another, knocking over a carefully stacked pile of firewood. Logs scattered across the stone floor with a loud clatter.

The monkey tensed, expecting the student who had been knocked to react with anger. But to his surprise, the student simply looked at the fallen logs, nodded once, and began restacking them without a word.

The monkey knitted his brow. *Why didn't they snap? Why didn't they scold the one who knocked them over?*

Curious—and agitated by the realization that *he* would have reacted with anger if his pile of logs had been knocked over—he turned toward the old master, who was seated nearby, calmly sipping tea.

"Master, why do I get so easily irritated? When things don't go my way, when someone insults me, when obstacles appear—I react before I even think! But that student... he just let it go! How?"

The master took a slow sip, his eyes calm. "Do you always have a choice in what happens to you?"

The monkey scowled. "No! That's the problem. Life throws things at me, and I... react!"

The master nodded thoughtfully. Then, without warning, he tipped his tea cup over, spilling the warm liquid onto the stone steps. The monkey leapt up, his eyes wide.

"Master! You've spilled your tea!"

The master remained still, watching as the liquid seeped into the cracks of the stone. Then, he turned to the monkey. "Did I react?"

The monkey hesitated. "No... but why didn't you? It was your tea."

The master smiled. "Because my reaction would not change what had already happened."

The monkey frowned, eyes narrowing. "But that's different! If someone insults me or does something unfair, how can I not react?"

The master rose and strolled into the temple. When he returned, he carried a beautiful porcelain vase. "Hold this," he said, placing it in the monkey's hands.

The monkey took the vase, eyeing the master warily.

Then, without warning, the master flicked the monkey's forehead.

"Ow!" the monkey cried, nearly dropping the vase. His eyes flashed with annoyance. "Why did you do that?"

The master chuckled. "What did you almost do just now?"

"I almost dropped the vase!"

The master nodded. "And why didn't you?"

The monkey huffed. "Because I chose not to! I didn't want to break it."

The master's smile deepened. "Ah. So, you can choose whether to react or not."

The monkey's mouth fell open. "You cheated!" he protested, "It's not the same!" But as he looked down at the vase in his hands, the weight of understanding settled upon him.

"So... I can do the same with my emotions?"

The master nodded. "You just proved it to yourself."

The monkey's ears twitched. *I caught the reaction before it broke something. I chose to protect the vase. I can choose to protect my peace too.*

The master continued, "When you react, you let yourself be pulled off balance. You let the world dictate your emotions. But when you choose how you respond, just as you protected the vase, you can also protect your peace."

The monkey turned the vase in his hands, mulling over the insight. "So... when someone insults me, I don't have to react? I can choose my response?"

The master nodded. "And in that choice, you find freedom."

The monkey let out a slow breath, but... *could it really be that simple?* His whole life, he had reacted without thinking—like a flame catching fire at the slightest spark. Could he truly learn to respond instead?

His old self fought against the idea. *But what if they deserve my anger? What if reacting is the only way to show strength?*

He wanted to believe the master.

He placed the vase beside him and sat back down, staring at the spilled tea, the master, the sky above. The lesson made sense, but deep inside, even with everything he'd learned, he wasn't sure he could live it.

For now, the battle within him remained—an old habit refusing to loosen its grip. But as he sat in the quiet, watching the last drops of tea vanish into the stone, he wondered... *What if strength was not in the reaction, but in the space between the impulse and the choice?*

Pause & Reflect

Have you ever mistaken reaction for strength? If you paused before reacting, what might change in your interactions with others—and within yourself?

Chapter 14
The Hidden Gift of Synchronicity

The wandering monkey trudged through the thick underbrush, flailing his arms dramatically to show his irritation. His search had turned up nothing.

For days, he had been trying to find a particular tree—one the master had once mentioned, said to bear the sweetest fruit in the valley. But each time he thought he was close, the path twisted, the landmarks blurred, and the forest seemed to shift like a trickster playing games.

He wiped sweat from his brow and scowled. "Ridiculous," he muttered. "I've come all this way, and for what? Nothing."

His stomach growled, annoying him even more. He could have stayed at the temple, eaten his usual meal, and avoided this entire mess. Instead, here he was, chasing after something he wasn't even sure existed.

He let out an exasperated sigh and sat on a fallen log, rubbing his temples. Just as he did, a voice broke the silence.

"Seems like you've lost your way."

The monkey jerked his head up. Across from him, half-hidden by the dappled shadows of the trees, sat an elder monkey—one he had never seen before. His fur was silvered with age. A long, gnarled staff rested across his lap.

"Who are you?" the wandering monkey asked warily.

The old monkey smiled. "Just another traveler." He tilted his head. "What are you looking for?"

The younger monkey hesitated, suddenly feeling foolish. "A tree," he muttered. "One that's supposed to have the sweetest fruit in the valley. But I think I've wasted my time."

The elder raised an eyebrow. "And yet, here you are."

The monkey rolled his eyes. "Yes, here I am. Hungry, lost, and empty-handed."

The old monkey chortled, unfazed.

"Tell me," he said, tapping his staff against the ground, "have you ever heard the story of the two travelers?"

The younger monkey shook his head. "Does it have anything to do with finding my way out of here?"

The elder ignored the sarcasm in his voice and continued, leaning back against the trunk of a tree.

"Long ago, there were two travelers searching for a hidden spring—one said to hold the purest water in the land. The first traveler was meticulous. He mapped out his route, measured distances, and insisted on following a precise plan. But no matter how much he strategized, he never found the spring."

"The second traveler?"

The elder's eyes twinkled. "He followed something else.

"A butterfly fluttering just ahead, as if waiting for him to follow.

"A sudden breeze carrying the scent of fresh water.

"A deer drinking from a tiny stream—one that led to a greater source.

"He followed the clues life placed before him, instead of forcing his own way. And eventually… he found the spring."

The younger monkey huffed. "So, what? He didn't find the spring… it found him?"

The elder chuckled. "You could say that. Or you could say that he noticed what was already there."

The monkey rolled his eyes again. "And how am I supposed to know which signs are real and which are just random noise?"

The elder smiled. "You don't always. But you notice. You listen. And sometimes, just by paying attention, you end up exactly where you need to be."

The younger monkey grumbled under his breath, waving a hand dismissively. But before he could turn away, the elder casually pointed with his staff.

The monkey's eyes followed—and his breath caught.

There, just beyond a bend in the path, was the tree.

His mind reeled. *Had it been there this whole time? Had he stormed right past it in his frustration?*

He gasped. *If the older monkey hadn't stopped him… would he have ever noticed?*

He looked at the tree. Then at the elder.

The awareness hit him like a gust of wind.

The lesson wasn't just the story. The lesson was happening to me.

The elder chuckled. "Perhaps you weren't lost at all. Perhaps you were just meant to see it… now."

The monkey swallowed. "That's just a coincidence."

The elder smiled, tapping his staff lightly against the earth. "Perhaps. Or perhaps not."

A soft breeze stirred the leaves. Somewhere in the distance, a bird called.

The monkey's tail curled slightly.

How many things he had dismissed as chance—when maybe, all along, they were signs waiting for him to notice?

Pause & Reflect

How often do you dismiss something as "just a coincidence" instead of seeing it as a clue? Have you ever rushed past an opportunity, only to realize later that the signs were there all along?

Chapter 15
Boredom: A Doorway to Insight

The wandering monkey sprawled across the temple steps, staring intently at the sky. His fingers drummed against the warm stone, his tail flicking with restless energy. The warm afternoon breeze rustled the trees, carrying the scent of blooming honeysuckle, but he barely noticed.

He was bored.

And worse—he was stuck with it.

He had already spent the morning balancing on the temple walls, sweeping the courtyard, counting the koi fish in the pond. And yet, no matter how many things he did, the restless itch beneath his skin refused to fade. The students had gone off to meditate, the master had vanished to who-knows-where, and now there was nothing left to do.

Then as if struck by a brilliant idea, he sat up suddenly to look around. His mind churned with "shoulds." *I should be practicing something. Learning something. Doing something. What good is a wasted afternoon?*

He sighed theatrically, flopping onto his back again. Maybe if he stared at the sky long enough, something interesting would happen.

Just then, the old master appeared from the temple, carrying a bundle of firewood. He paused when he saw the monkey lying there like a discarded rag.

The master set down the wood with a thud. "Is the sky offering answers today?"

The monkey groaned, covering his face. "No, Master. The sky is just as dull as everything else."

The master sat beside him. "So, you suffer."

The monkey peeked through his fingers. "I don't *suffer*. I'm just *bored*."

The master nodded. "Ah. A terrible thing, boredom."

The monkey sat up quickly. "*Yes!* It is! There's nothing to do, nothing to learn, nothing *happening!* It's unbearable."

The master nodded solemnly. "Come with me."

The monkey's ears perked up. *Finally,* something. He scrambled to his feet and followed the master through the temple gardens, past the cherry blossoms, the winding stone paths, the silent meditation halls.

At last, they arrived at a small wooden door hidden at the back of the temple. The master pushed it open, revealing a dim, empty room.

The monkey squinted. "What is this place?"

The master stepped inside and gestured for the monkey to follow. The room was windowless, silent, and completely bare except for a single cushion in the center.

"This," the master said, "is the Room of Nothing."

The monkey wrinkled his nose. "That sounds *boring*."

The master chuckled. "Indeed. That is why you will sit here for a while."

The monkey's eyes widened. "Sit here? *Doing nothing?*"

The master nodded. "Yes. Do not move, do not seek distraction, do not fight the boredom. Simply be with it."

The monkey groaned but obeyed, collapsing onto the cushion. The master left, closing the door behind him.

The darkness was absolute.

Not the soft, familiar darkness of twilight or the comforting shadows beneath the trees. This was different—a vast, weighty absence of light, of movement, of anything beyond himself.

At first, the monkey sat stiffly, arms folded, tail twitching. He tried to embrace the moment, as the master had suggested, but there was only disorientation. Without sight, his other senses reached outward, grasping for something—a flicker, a whisper, a point of reference.

There was nothing.

He blinked, but it made no difference.

For a moment, his body tensed—not in fear, but in resistance. His mind, unanchored by sight, searched hard for something to hold onto—a sound, a shape, the faintest glow.

And still, there was only stillness.

Then his mind spun in protest. This was ridiculous. He could be doing *anything* else—climbing trees, talking to the master, even sweeping the courtyard again. He thought about his journey since leaving his old jungle, the lessons he had learned, the things he still wanted to know. Then...

I should meditate.

I should practice mindfulness.

I should... stop thinking about what I should do.

He sighed dramatically. He had never sat this long doing absolutely nothing.

His tail curled and uncurled. He tapped his fingers against his knee. Sighed. Shifted his weight once, then twice, then five more times just to see if it felt any different.

And then came the deeper doubts.

What if I've been tricked? What if the master just needed a break and put me in here so he could take a nap?

He huffed. He scratched his ear. He counted his breaths.

One, two, three, four—how long have I been here?

It had to have been hours. Maybe even days.

He rolled his eyes.

But nothing helped.

Boredom sat on his chest, heavy and unyielding.

Fine. FINE. I'll just... be still.

He let out another loud exaggerated sigh, as if that would bring the master back, even though he knew it wouldn't.

Finally, he resigned himself to his fate.

And just sat. For aeons. Or so it seemed.

Then—

Something strange happened.

His thoughts began to slow... and his awareness turned inward.

He could hear his own breath—steady, rhythmic, and impossibly loud. The faint rustle of fur as he shifted. The softest echo of his movements against the unseen walls.

And then, like eyes adjusting to the night, he began to settle into it.

He noticed the way the silence had a texture—soft, gentle, like the hush of a distant sea. He became aware of the tiny details he had always missed—the faint scent of old wood, the reassuringly calm pulse of his own heartbeat—of life moving in the stillness. The air was neither warm nor cool, just... there, holding him in its quiet embrace.

The boredom had melted into something else.

Stillness.

Clarity.

Presence.

He didn't know how long he had been sitting there when the door finally creaked open. The master stood in the doorway, smiling.

"Well?" the master asked.

The monkey blinked, as if waking from a dream. "It... wasn't as bad as I thought."

The master smiled. "Indeed. You see, little one, boredom is not an enemy. It is a doorway. When you stop running from it, you enter a space where the mind quiets, and awareness deepens. It is not the lack of something—it is the presence of everything."

The monkey looked down at his hands. He had spent much of his life chasing distractions, filling time with noise, movement, tasks. He had never once stopped to see what lay beyond boredom—beyond the need to be entertained, occupied, or *doing*.

"I never knew doing nothing could feel like... *something*," the monkey admitted. So much of his journey had been seeking—searching for the next lesson, the next answer, the next moment to fill. But here, in the silence, he had found something without needing to chase it at all.

The master laughed softly. "When the mind stops searching, it finds. Not through effort, but through presence."

The monkey stepped out of the dark room, back into the golden light of the garden. But this time, everything looked different—the cherry blossoms were more vibrant, the air felt crisper, the sounds of the birds clearer.

But it wasn't the world that was different.

It was him.

He had glimpsed something beyond boredom.

Could he truly sit with stillness again?

Only time would tell.

Pause & Reflect

How often do you fill the empty spaces in your life with noise, distractions, or movement? What would happen if you allowed yourself to sit with stillness, without trying to change it? Could boredom be an invitation to something deeper?

Chapter 16
The Wild Freedom of No Goals

Days flew by, and today, the wandering monkey sat near the temple courtyard, watching as the students practiced their disciplines. Some moved gracefully through martial arts forms, others traced symbols onto parchment with delicate strokes. But it was the archers that held his attention.

They stood in perfect stillness, bows raised, eyes locked on distant targets. One by one, arrows sailed through the air, some striking their mark with precision, others falling just short. But no one seemed discouraged. They simply drew, aimed, and released once more.

The monkey frowned. *They all have a goal. Something to master, something to achieve.*

He looked down at his hands. *But what about me?*

He was always wandering. Always questioning. Always seeking. He had no single skill, no target to hit, no final destination to reach.

And wasn't that... *wrong*?

He felt a familiar tension creep in—a restlessness, a quiet fear that he was getting it all wrong. That he should be striving harder, focusing on something specific, working toward something concrete.

As if sensing his thoughts, the archery master glanced over. "Would you like to try?" he asked.

The monkey hesitated. He had never drawn a bow before, but something in the master's voice—steady, inviting, free of expectation—made him nod.

The master handed him a bow, adjusting his stance. "Draw the string," he instructed. The monkey pulled it back awkwardly. "Now aim."

The monkey squinted at the target in the distance.

"Wait." The master's voice stopped him. "Do not aim with your eyes alone. Feel where the arrow wants to go."

The monkey tilted his head. That made no sense. An arrow needed direction. A goal. A target. Otherwise, it was just—

He let go. The arrow veered wide, disappearing into the grass.

A few students tittered. The monkey's face grew hot.

"I knew it," he muttered. "I have no direction. No goal. No skill. What's the point?"

The archery master studied him for a moment. Then he asked, "Tell me—do you believe these students are here because they set a goal to be archers?"

The monkey folded his arms. "Of course. How else would they get so good?"

The master smiled. "Let me show you something."

They left the archery range and walked down toward the temple pond, where koi fish swam lazily beneath the water's surface. The monkey recognized this place immediately.

He had been here before. He had spoken with the temple master about goals. He had resisted the lesson then.

The master knelt by the water's edge. "Watch them," he said.

The koi glided effortlessly, shifting with the current, weaving between one another, their movements fluid and unforced.

"They move, they explore, they live," the master continued. "But tell me—do they seem lost? Are they wasting their time because they are not chasing something?"

The monkey hesitated, still unsure about the idea of *no goals*.

The master tossed a small pebble into the water. Ripples spread outward in perfect circles.

"The students you saw today did not become archers because they set a goal. They simply loved the feel of the bow in their hands, the pull of the string, the flight of the arrow. It called to them, and so they followed."

The monkey watched as the ripples widened, then faded.

"You believe mastery comes from setting and chasing a goal," the master said, his voice gentle. "But what if it comes from being pulled toward something because of your love for it?"

The monkey frowned, his mind yielding to the idea but still resisting it at the same time.

No goals? How could that be right? It wasn't the way of the world as he had known it.

How could letting go of goals possibly lead anywhere?

Yet, as he watched the koi swim, as he felt the memory of the bow in his hands, something struck a new chord.

He still didn't fully understand.

But maybe—just maybe—there was more to this than he had once thought.

And for now, that was enough.

Pause & Reflect

Where in your life have you clung to goals because you believed they were necessary? What if true mastery comes not from chasing but from being pulled toward what naturally moves you?

Chapter 17
The Flow of Having Enough

The wandering monkey sat beneath the shade of a mango tree, staring at the golden fruit hanging from its branches. A warm breeze stirred the leaves, carrying the scent of ripened sweetness and the distant sounds of temple students practicing their martial arts.

It should have been a peaceful moment.

He had eaten. His stomach was full. His body was content.

And yet, his mind was not.

His tail curled tighter. His fingers dug into the earth.

I should gather more.

The thought rose instinctively, even though he knew he didn't need to.

What if I don't have enough tomorrow? What if something happens? What if I wake up one day, and there is nothing left?

The old fear pressed against his ribs, familiar and unshakable.

He *knew* this lesson. He had heard the master's words before.

And yet...

His jaw tightened. *Why does it still feel real?*

Hadn't he learned? Hadn't he changed?

The monkey sighed and let his head fall back against the tree.

His thoughts were a battle within him—one part remembering the truth, the other clinging to old beliefs like a vine refusing to let go of a dying tree.

His chest tightened. *What if none of the master's words were ever real?*

Hadn't he seen it yesterday at mealtime? He and another student had both rushed for the last banana, a split-second of competition had overtaken reason, his mind had whispered, *If I don't take it now, I might not get another chance.*

He had seen it in himself. He had seen it in others.

Lack was real. It existed.

He couldn't simply pretend it wasn't there.

A rustling nearby pulled him from his thoughts. The old master approached, settling beside him. He did not speak right away. He simply sat, his presence as steady as the trees around them, waiting.

Finally, the master said, "You are troubled."

The monkey clenched his jaw. The words tumbled out, raw and unfiltered.

"Why do I always feel like I need more?" His voice was sharp with chagrin. "More food, more answers, more control? Even when I have enough, I don't feel like I do. I thought I was learning. I thought I was changing. But here I am, stuck in the same old fears."

The master nodded, unshaken by the storm in the monkey's heart. He reached up, plucked a single mango from the tree, and placed it in the monkey's hands.

"Tell me, little one. If you take a drink from the river, how much water do you need?"

The monkey blinked, gripping the mango too tightly. "Just enough to quench my thirst."

The master nodded. "And do you need to take more, just in case the river disappears tomorrow?"

The monkey snorted indignantly. "No. The river is always flowing."

The master chuckled. "Then why do you worry about having enough?"

The monkey sat up straighter, his tail snapping against the ground.

"Because... because what if one day, it doesn't flow?" The words tasted bitter in his mouth. He looked away, ashamed of his own doubt. "What if the tree stops bearing fruit? What if I wake up, and there isn't enough?"

The master studied him for a long moment, then gestured toward the tree. "Look at the branches."

The monkey glanced up. The tree was full of mangoes, but not all of them were ripe. Some were still green, waiting for their time. Others had already fallen, given freely to the earth below.

"The tree does not rush to bear all fruit at once," the master said. "It does not hoard in fear of the future. It simply grows, allowing each mango to ripen in its own time. And then, next season, does it not bear fruit again?"

The monkey swallowed. "But what if I am different? What if I need to hold on, just in case?"

The master's smile softened. "Ah. And has holding on ever made you feel truly safe?"

The monkey deliberated.

He thought of the last banana at mealtime. The way he had rushed to take it, fearing there wouldn't be another chance.

Had that made him feel more secure?

Had it brought peace?

Or had it just made him feel smaller?

The answer sat heavy in his chest.

"No," he admitted, his voice barely above a whisper.

The master's smile deepened. "Then perhaps, little one, it is not more that you seek, but the trust that what you have is already enough."

The monkey looked down at the mango in his hands.

It was whole, perfect, ripe now. Not tomorrow. Not yesterday. *Now.*

Had enough ever been about what he had?

Or had it always been about what he believed?

His grip loosened. The tension in his chest softened.

The tree did not fear lack.

The river did not question its flow.

And perhaps he didn't have to either.

He took a slow breath, the knot inside of him unwinding.

"So, enough isn't about how much I have—it's about knowing I don't need more than this moment gives me?"

The master smiled. "Yes, little one. Enough is not a number. It is a *feeling*."

The monkey lifted the mango to his lips, taking a bite.

The sweetness filled his mouth, rich and full.

He had eaten mangoes before, but never had one tasted like this—like complete satisfaction, like peace, like the filling of a gap within he had never realized was there.

For the first time in his life, he did not feel the need to reach for more.

But as he sat beneath the tree, his tail flicked thoughtfully.

"Master," he said slowly, "but what if the tree did stop bearing fruit? What if one day, the river did not flow? Should I still do nothing?"

The master laughed softly. "Ah, little one. *Do nothing?*" He shook his head. "No. A fisherman casts his net when the time is right. A bird gathers twigs to build a nest before the rains come. Even the tree sends its roots deeper when the dry season arrives.

"Action has its place. But only a fool plucks a fruit before it is ripe or casts his net in an empty stream."

The monkey let the words settle in.

His fear had never been about whether to act—it had been about acting from fear itself.

Why had he spent so long clinging, striving, preparing for a future that had not yet come, that he had forgotten to trust the rhythm of things?

Action was not the enemy.

Forcing, striving, and hoarding in fear—that was the burden.

The master stood, ready to leave.

"Ah, little one. When you stop fearing lack, you will see—life has always been enough."

A fresh mango fell naturally from the tree, landing beside the monkey with a soft thud.

He smiled, watching the way it had come to him—not from reaching, not from striving, not from fear—but simply, because it was time.

Pause & Reflect

Where in your life do you fear not having enough—whether it's time, love, security, or success? What would change if you trusted that life will always provide exactly what you need, when you need it?

Chapter 18
The Paradox of Striving

The wandering monkey sat on the temple steps, rolling a small stone between his fingers.

Several weeks had passed. His mind, for once, was not racing ahead or clinging to old frustrations. Instead, it hovered in an unfamiliar place—somewhere between understanding and doubt.

His last realization had been real. He had felt it settle deep in his bones, the quiet ease of not grasping so tightly. And yet, another part of him still whispered:

What if I slip back?

What if, after all this, I still fall into my old ways?

He let out a slow breath and looked up at the sky, watching the clouds drift—without force, without direction, yet always moving.

A small sound nearby broke his reverie—the quiet, rhythmic clink of stone against wood.

He turned his head.

A young temple student sat a short distance away, his hands moving with effortless precision, balancing stones on a thin bamboo rod.

The monkey's breath caught.

He had seen the master do this before—a feat of graceful control, balance without effort. It had seemed impossible then. It seemed impossible now.

And yet, here was a student—not a master, not a teacher, but just another learner like himself—doing it with such ease.

The student glanced up, caught the monkey's stare, and grinned. "Want to try?"

The monkey hesitated. He didn't want to look stupid. But something about the invitation—felt important.

He scampered over. The student handed him a bamboo rod and a small, smooth stone. "It's simple," he said. "Just balance it."

The monkey smirked. *Simple? Right.*

He gripped the bamboo tightly, bracing himself. He placed the stone on top.

It wobbled. He squeezed harder.

The stone toppled.

The student laughed, amused. "Try again."

The monkey narrowed his eyes and adjusted his grip. This time, he focused all his attention, stiffening his arms, locking his muscles.

The stone wobbled. He clenched his jaw, holding his breath.

The stone fell again.

Frustration flared. The monkey gritted his teeth. "This is ridiculous. How are you doing that so easily?"

The student shrugged. "I'm not *doing* it. I'm just letting it happen."

The monkey's tail flicked. *Letting it happen? That didn't make sense.*

He grabbed the bamboo again. "I'll get it this time."

He braced himself, ready to hold completely still.

The student shook his head. "You're fighting it."

"I *have* to," the monkey snapped. "How else do I make it stay?"

The student simply smiled and tapped the bamboo stick lightly. The monkey watched as the stone wobbled but didn't fall.

The student was holding the stick—but not gripping it.

He was moving with the balance—not forcing it.

The monkey's mind flashed back to something else—a different moment, by the river, when the master had once asked him:

"If you try to hold water in your hands by squeezing tightly, what happens?"

The answer had been simple: It slips through your fingers.

He drew a sharp breath.

This was the same.

It wasn't about control. It wasn't about force.

It was about trusting the balance that was already there.

The monkey took a slow breath and tried again.

This time, he didn't grip the stick like a weapon. He held it lightly, his breath steady.

No forcing. No fighting. Just allowing.

The stone swayed—but it stayed.

His grip remained loose but sure.

A slow realization unfurled inside him.

Balance isn't stillness; it's a dance of constant motion.

The paradox struck him like a wave—the harder he tried, the more he failed.

But when he trusted, when he stopped resisting, stopped overthinking, stopped grasping—

The balance found him.

For the first time, the stone did not fall.

And neither did he.

A small smile tugged at the corners of his mouth.

The lesson he had resisted was beginning to take shape—not just in his mind, but in his hands, in his breath, in his way of being.

He wasn't trying to change anymore.

He was simply allowing it to happen.

And that... *that* was new.

Pause & Reflect

Where in your life have you been trying too hard to force an outcome? Could the very effort that's keeping you stuck be the thing you need to release?

Something for You – Free Zen-Inspired Gifts

The wisdom in *The Monkey and the Way of Zen* isn't just to be read—it's to be experienced. To support your journey beyond these pages, I've prepared a collection of gentle offerings:

☐ **The Monkey's Zen Companion** – A quick guide to the core Zen teaching behind each story.
☐ **The Dance of Coming Home** – An exclusive short story with one final conversation between the monkey and the master.
☐ **The Art of Gentle Presence** – Five simple, 2-minute practices to quiet overthinking and find peace.
☐ **The Way of the Quiet Mind** – A meditation guide with recorded practices to embody the book's lessons.
☐ **Reflections from the Monkey's Journey** – 6 mobile phone wallpapers featuring inspiring quotes from the stories.

These gifts are yours. May they remind you of the stillness beneath the noise, the space between the stories, and the infinite sky within.

Download your free gifts here:
https://bonuses.serenachoo.com/monkey-zen-unlock-your-bonuses/ or scan the QR code.

Chapter 19
The Weightless Freedom of Letting Go

The wandering monkey climbed the steep mountain path, his fingers tightly curled around a small gemstone—a deep blue sapphire he had found glistening in the riverbed far below.

It was the most beautiful thing he had ever seen. Smooth and cool in his palm, it sparkled even in the dim light.

"*This must be a sign,*" he told himself. "*Something so rare, so precious—I cannot let it go.*"

Yet beneath the awe, something gnawed at him.

He had learned much in his time at the temple. He had begun to trust life, to see how things flowed when he did not fight them.

But this... *this* was different.

This was something *tangible*, something *valuable*. Surely, this was worth holding onto?

Still, the climb was difficult. The path was narrow, the rocks uneven, and the wind howled against the mountainside. He climbed carefully, but with one hand always curled around the sapphire, every step became a struggle.

At one point, he reached for a sturdy branch to pull himself up—but with only one free hand, he slipped.

His stomach lurched. He barely caught himself in time, his heart hammering against his ribs.

Yet, even in that moment of fear, he refused to drop the gemstone.

No. His jaw tightened. *I can manage. I just have to try harder.*

But the effort drained him. His muscles ached, his breath came short, and his pace slowed to a crawl.

By the time he reached the temple, his legs felt like rocks, his fingers were scraped raw—but he still clung to the sapphire, cradling it like a prize.

"Master," he gasped, "look what I found!"

The master glanced at the monkey's outstretched hand.

"Ah, a sapphire. Very beautiful."

The monkey waited, his chest still rising and falling with exhaustion. He expected praise, acknowledgment, something to justify the effort he had spent protecting his treasure.

But the master simply continued sharpening his blade.

The silence stretched.

Finally, the master spoke. "Tell me, little one—did the sapphire make your journey easier?"

The monkey frowned with disappointment. "No... It made it harder."

The master nodded, still focused on his blade. "And if you had let it go?"

The monkey paused, his disappointment deepening. "I would have climbed faster. I wouldn't have struggled so much. But, Master, this is a rare gemstone! I may never find another like it."

The master smiled and set his blade aside. "Come."

He led the monkey to the temple garden, where a clear pond reflected the sky. The master bent down and picked up a stone from the water. He examined it for a moment, then casually tossed it back in.

Ripples spread outward, then faded into stillness.

"Did I lose anything?" the master asked.

The monkey blinked. "Well... the stone is gone."

Echoes of a distant lesson whispered in his mind. *Was this going to be about the fear of lack again?*

The master chuckled. "Was it ever mine to keep?"

The monkey looked down at the sapphire in his palm. Its surface was warm now, heated from his grasp.

"I don't understand."

The master continued, "You believe this stone is rare because you do not yet see how much life provides. You cling to it as if it defines your fortune. But in truth, it has only made your journey more difficult."

The monkey tightened his grip, the stone pressing into his skin.

He *knew* the master was right.

He had *felt* the weight of carrying it.

But still...

It was *his*.

What if he never found something like it again?

What if letting go meant missing out?

His breath grew shallow. His mind spun, whispering old fears. *If I don't hold on, what if I regret it? What if I lose something I can never replace?*

The master's voice was gentle. "Letting go is not losing, little one. It is opening. A hand clenched around one treasure cannot receive another. A mind filled with fear has no room for wisdom. A heart that grips too tightly forgets how to love."

The monkey stared at the gemstone, his pulse drumming in his ears.

It was just a rock. He knew this.

But could he really let it slip away so easily? He had climbed with it. Suffered for it. Held it through struggle and pain, sacrificed comfort for it. If he let it go now... what had all of that been for?

His fingers curled tightly around it, trembling.

Then—

He exhaled.

A deep, slow breath.

And before he could think, before he could stop himself—his fingers loosened, followed quickly by a slight hesitation and hint of resistance. Then—the sapphire slipped from his grasp, landing in the pond with a quiet splash.

The water swallowed it in an instant. A ripple spread outward before fading into stillness.

The monkey flexed his fingers, watching as the ripple faded.

He felt… lighter.

He had spent so much energy protecting the sapphire. But now, he felt something even more valuable—

Freedom.

As they walked back to the temple, the monkey noticed the world around him in a way he hadn't before—the scent of the flowers, the way the wind danced through the trees, the warmth of the sun on his fur.

And then—

Something glimmered at the edge of the path.

Another gemstone, half-buried in the earth.

The monkey paused, staring at it.

The master smiled knowingly.

"You see, little one, when you stop clinging to one treasure, you see how much more life offers."

The monkey laughed, shaking his head.

He did not reach for the new gemstone.

He simply kept walking.

The path stretched ahead, open and endless.

And now, he wasn't carrying anything at all.

Pause & Reflect

What would happen if you let go—not in loss, but in trust? Could releasing what no longer serves you open space for something greater?

Chapter 20
The Gentle Wisdom of Not Knowing

The next morning, the wandering monkey strolled through the temple gardens, hands clasped behind his back, his thoughts swirling like leaves caught in the wind.

He had let go of the sapphire.

He had felt the weight lift, the lightness of release.

And yet... he felt disconcerted.

Why had it been so difficult to let go?

He had believed the sapphire itself was important. But now, he saw the truth—the stone had never mattered.

It wasn't about the stone. It was about what it represented.

Certainty.

Security.

Knowing.

The comfort of having something solid in his grasp.

Letting go had not just meant surrendering an object—it had meant surrendering control.

And without control, he was left with something far more uncomfortable than holding on:

Not knowing.

His chest tightened.

His whole life, he had sought understanding, believing knowledge would bring safety. The more he understood, the more control he would have. But now, the more he learned, the more he saw how little he actually knew.

And that... was *terrifying*.

Lost in thought, he nearly walked past the temple gardener—an older monkey, kneeling in the dirt, hands dusted with soil as he tended to a row of small sprouts. The monkey stopped, watching as the gardener worked, his movements steady and unhurried.

Something about the way he moved made the monkey pause.

After a moment, he put out his palm, displaying a small seed he had picked up earlier. He frowned at it, then glanced at the gardener.

"Do you know what this is?"

The gardener took the seed between his fingers, examining it with curious ease, then handed it back with a small smile.

"I don't know."

The monkey raised his eyebrows in surprise. "You don't?"

The gardener shook his head. "Should I?"

The monkey blinked. "Well... you work in the gardens. You plant things. You must know a lot about seeds."

The gardener laughed, amused. "I do. But that doesn't mean I know this one."

The monkey frowned. That didn't feel like a real answer.

He rolled the seed between his fingers again. "Not knowing makes me uncomfortable," he admitted. "I like to be prepared."

The gardener nodded, his hands still working the soil. "Then tell me, what do you plan to do with it?"

The monkey hesitated. "I suppose I could plant it."

The gardener gestured toward an open patch of soft earth. "Go ahead."

The monkey dug a small hole and placed the seed inside, covering it gently with soil. He patted it flat, then stared at the spot expectantly.

A moment passed.

Nothing happened.

He glanced up. "Now what?"

The gardener raised an eyebrow. "What do you mean?"

The monkey gestured impatiently at the dirt. "How do I know if it's growing? When will it sprout?"

The gardener smiled. "Do you believe that staring at it will make it grow faster?"

The monkey sighed. "No, but... what if it never grows? What if it was a bad seed?"

The gardener sat back, dusting his hands off. "And what if it wasn't?"

The monkey frowned. "But what if—"

The gardener held up a hand. "Do you believe that a seed knows exactly when it will sprout?"

The monkey hesitated. "...No?"

The gardener nodded. "Neither do you. And yet, the seed doesn't worry. It doesn't demand certainty. It simply rests in the soil until the time is right."

Until the time is right.

An old lesson with the master echoed in the monkey's mind. *Trusting what cannot yet be seen.*

He looked down at the fresh patch of dirt.

He had no control over it now.

It would sprout, or it wouldn't. It would grow, or it wouldn't. No amount of thinking about it would change that.

A thought arose inside him. *How many times had he exhausted himself trying to answer questions that did not need answering, trying to figure out things that were not his to solve?*

He had worried about things beyond his reach, things that would unfold with or without his intervention—like the passing of seasons, the flow of the river, or whether a seed would sprout.

The gardener stood, adjusting his woven hat. "You fear not knowing because you believe you need to know. But what if not knowing is simply part of the way things unfold?"

The monkey let the words settle in.

The unknown was not a problem to be solved.

Maybe the seed would sprout. Maybe it wouldn't. Maybe the rains would come. Maybe they wouldn't.

And maybe... that was okay.

The monkey dusted off his hands and stood, resisting the urge to glance back at the soil.

He didn't need to check.

And he was at peace with that.

Pause & Reflect

Where in your life are you waiting for certainty before moving forward? What would happen if you let go of needing to know everything right now?

Chapter 21
The Space Between Stories

The wandering monkey sat beneath the vast canopy of the jungle, watching the golden hues of the setting sun flicker through the swaying leaves. The evening air was filled with the woody aroma of drenched bark after the rain, while the rhythmic hum of cicadas filled the silence between rustling branches.

A gentle breeze rippled across the river, making the water dance in shifting patterns of silver and shadow.

As he watched the river's endless flow, his ears perked up. The water seemed to whisper stories—of raindrops that had once fallen from distant clouds, of streams that had carried them here, of the long journey still ahead.

Stories were everywhere—

In the chants of the temple students,
In the whispers of the jungle trees,
In the lessons of the old master.

And in his own mind.

He told himself stories all the time.

Stories about who he was.
Stories about what he should be.
Stories about why things happened the way they did.

Some stories made him feel proud.
Some made him feel small.
Some made him doubt everything he thought he knew.

And tonight, he was caught in one again.

I should be wiser by now. Haven't I learned this lesson before? Yet here I am, caught in the same doubts, the same thoughts circling endlessly. The master must think I'm slow... Maybe I am. Maybe I will always be chasing understanding, never truly grasping it.

The thoughts tangled together like vines, tightening their grip, refusing to let go.

Yeah, yeah, spiral of growth and all that.

He barely noticed the master approaching until his voice cut through the noise.

"Ah, little one. You are lost in a forest of your own making."

The monkey looked up and let out a heavy sigh. "I know my mind weaves stories, and I've learned not to believe them all but..." He rubbed his temples, as his voice trailed off.

Looking down, he whispered, "They still pull me in."

The master sat beside him, gazing at the horizon. "Ah, yes. Stories... but tell me, where does one story end and the next begin?"

The monkey looked up, perplexed. *What was the master saying?*

A story felt solid, like a path you could walk on. *But... was it?*

He hesitated. *Hold on...*

If he really looked closely, there were moments—tiny, fleeting pauses—where one thought ended before the next began. *Was he imagining it?*

Is that what the master meant?

The master continued, "Most creatures believe they are the stories in their minds. But have you ever noticed the space between them?"

The monkey tilted his head.

The master gestured to the sky, then to the river.

"Between the stars, there is space... between the waves, there is still water."

He tapped the monkey's forehead lightly. "And between thoughts, there is silence."

For a second, the monkey let his mind settle.

Then in that brief moment, he saw it again—

There was *space*.

Between one worry and the next, there was a brief pause.
Between one self-judgment and another, there was emptiness.

It was so subtle, he almost missed it—a silence that had always been there... but that he had never noticed before.

The master nodded, seeing understanding begin to dawn.

"That space, little one, is where you truly are. Not in the stories. Not in the thoughts. But in the stillness between them."

The monkey sat quietly.

I should be wiser by now.

He saw the thought appear—then a pause—then it faded.

The master must think I'm slow.

Another pause. Another gap.

As fleeting as they were, he had noticed.

For the first time, he was not trapped inside the stories.

He was *watching* them.

A slow smile spread across his face. "Master, it's quiet in the space between stories."

The master nodded. "Yes. And more than that, it is where wisdom is gathered."

The monkey frowned. "But how? If I am not my stories, what happens to everything I've learned? My struggles, my mistakes... wouldn't they be lost?"

The master chuckled. "Ah, little one. Do you think the river loses the rain that has fallen into it?"

The monkey blinked. "No... the water becomes part of the river."

"And so it is with you," the master said. "All that you have lived, all that you have struggled with, has already shaped you. It does not need to be retold for it to be known."

The monkey looked down at his hands. He had long clung to stories, believing they defined him.

But now, he wondered...

"If I no longer need the stories," he asked slowly, "does that mean they don't matter anymore? I love telling the temple students my stories."

The master smiled. "No, little one. But they will stop binding you. When wisdom is gathered, the stories no longer carry weight. They simply become tales to tell, like an old legend passed around a fire—without the need to relive them."

The monkey looked up at the sky, at the spaces between the stars. He watched the river, how the waves rose and fell, yet the water remained.

His stories would come and go, like passing clouds.

But in the space between them, he was free.

Not as the story of who he thought he was, but as the quiet presence beneath it all.

And for the first time, he felt it—

Not as an idea, but as something true.

Pause & Reflect

In your daily life, do you allow space between your thoughts, or do you fill every moment with mental noise? What happens when you notice the space between your thoughts instead of getting lost in them?

Chapter 22
The Boundless Lightness of Being

The wandering monkey moved through the jungle, his senses alive with the richness of the morning.

He felt the warmth of the *komorebi*—the soft sunlight that filtered through the canopy, dappling his fur in shifting patches of gold. The scent of blooming flowers drifted in the air, mingling with the crisp freshness of the breeze. Birds called from the treetops, their melodies weaving through the rustling leaves. Quiet reminders that even the smallest moments held beauty.

He leapt from branch to branch, his body moving effortlessly, instinctively. His mind, for once, was *still*.

He was not thinking.
He was not planning.
He was simply *being*.

And it felt... light.

Not just in his body—but in his mind.

He was not weighed down by questions or worries.
He was not tangled in thoughts of *what next?*
He was simply here, in the flow of the moment.

And then—

He slipped.

A loose branch snapped beneath his grip, and he plummeted straight down, crashing into a pile of soft leaves with a spectacular *flump*.

Laughter erupted nearby.

The monkey propped himself up to see a small group of temple students stood at the edge of the clearing, watching the monkey with amused curiosity. The master was with them. They had been passing through the jungle, gathering herbs for the temple kitchen.

One of the younger students guffawed. "What a fall!"

A short pause. Then he did something unexpected.

He laughed.

Not a nervous laugh. Not a frustrated one.

But a laugh of *pure, unshaken joy*.

And that's when it hit him.

Had this happened before, he would have been mortified, flustered, overthinking every second. He would have imagined the temple students snickering behind his back. He would have replayed the fall in his mind, picking apart every mistake.

He would have turned a simple stumble into *proof* that something was wrong with him.

But now?

There was none of that.

No weight. No burden of judgment.

It was just what it was.

And it was light.

The students exchanged glances. One of them stepped forward, tilting his head. "You're not upset?"

The monkey grinned, still sprawled on the leaves. "No..."

"Ah, little one. You have finally fallen without falling into yourself," came the master's voice, filled with a knowing smile.

The monkey grinned. "Master, I just fell... and for some reason, I don't feel bad about it."

The master chuckled. "Ah. And why do you think that is?"

The monkey scratched his head. "I think... it's because I didn't make it mean anything."

The master nodded. "Yes, little one. Life is not as serious as you believe it to be."

The monkey sat up, still brushing leaves from his fur. "But isn't life important?"

The master picked up a small rock and tossed it lightly into the air. "Yes. But importance does not mean heaviness."

The students gathered round.

The monkey frowned. "I don't get it."

The master suddenly puffed out his chest, puckered his brow, and stomped around in an exaggerated, lumbering march. "*I am the Great and Serious One!*" he bellowed in a ridiculously deep voice. "*Everything is Important! Every step must be measured! I must not stumble!*"

The entire group and the monkey burst into laughter.

The master stopped and grinned. "Exactly." He dusted off his robes. "You see, those who take themselves too seriously become rigid, heavy, burdened by their own importance. But life—life is meant to be *danced with, played with, moved through lightly.*"

The monkey exhaled, his smile widening. "So I can still care... but I don't have to carry?"

The master nodded. "Yes, little one. When you stop clinging to every moment as if it is a great test, you discover what life truly is—an experience, not a problem to be solved."

Some students nodded as they took in the master's words, others looked on in awe.

The monkey leaned back against the leaves, looking up at the sky. The clouds drifted easily, without direction or worry. The river flowed around rocks instead of fighting against them.

He had focused so much energy in the past on trying to be perfect, to get it all *right*, to hold himself to impossible standards.

But life was not a test, not something to be measured that way at all.

It was a *playground*. A *river*. A *dance*.

The master stretched. "Come, young ones, we must get back before the afternoon bells."

The students grinned, gathering their baskets.

The monkey waved, leapt into the trees, and swung once more—

No effort. No strain. No weight.

Only the *lightness of being*.

Pause & Reflect

Where in your life do you take things so seriously that they become a burden? What would change if you approached life with a little more lightness and play?

Chapter 23
The Stories We Weave (Revisited)

The late afternoon sun stretched long golden ribbons across the temple courtyard. A warm breeze carried the scent of burning incense from the temple, rustling the leaves of an old fig tree where the wandering monkey moved with quiet ease.

His fingers brushed the rough bark as he leapt to a lower branch, his body moving without thought. Below, the stone path shimmered with the heat of the day, its cracks filled with tiny sprouts of green—life finding a way in the smallest spaces.

Somewhere nearby, a bird trilled, its call bright and sharp against the hum of cicadas.

The monkey paused, closing his eyes.

There was nothing to do.

Nothing to solve.

No tangled thoughts pulling at him.

Just the warmth of the sun on his fur. The steady rhythm of his breath. The world, as it was.

A day of pure ease.

Then—

Laughter.

The monkey's ears twitched.

He opened his eyes and glanced down.

A small group of temple students sat near the fountain, whispering between giggles before breaking into another burst of quiet laughter.

Something stirred inside him. A flicker of thought—

"Are they laughing at me?"

A sharp pang. A familiar tightening in his chest.

The urge to react.

It was an old thought. An old story.

One he had once believed without question.

But now—

He didn't grab hold of it.

He simply noticed it—like a leaf floating past on the breeze.

It was there, but it wasn't his.

The students laughed again, and this time, he simply listened.

It was light. Playful. It had nothing to do with him.

A breath escaped him, long and deep.

How many times have I carried stories that were never mine to begin with?

Footsteps approached.

One of the older students, carrying a small basket of ripe plums, paused beside the monkey's tree. "You're quiet today."

The monkey blinked, still lingering in the moment. "I almost believed something that wasn't real."

The student tilted his head, curious. "What do you mean?"

The monkey looked toward the fountain, where the laughter continued, carrying no weight, no hidden meaning.

"I used to think every laugh, every glance, every whisper had something to do with me," he said slowly.

The student smirked. "Sounds exhausting."

The monkey chuckled. "It was. I would try and figure out which stories were real and which weren't, but now... I see that *none* of them are me."

The student sat beneath the tree, setting the basket beside him. He picked up a plum, turning it over in his hand. "You know," he mused, "I used to worry all the time about how people saw me. If someone frowned, I thought it meant they were upset with me. If they didn't greet me, I thought I had done something wrong."

He tossed the plum lightly in the air, catching it with ease. "But one day, I realized something. People are living their own stories, too. Most of the time, their thoughts have nothing to do with us at all."

The monkey's tail curled slightly.

Yes. Yes.

That was it.

All this time, he had been weaving himself into other people's stories, believing their laughter, their moods, their passing expressions had something to do with him.

When in truth—

They were simply busy with their own lives—and their own thoughts.

The monkey glanced towards the sky, where the golden light flickered between the branches.

His thoughts had always told him who he was.

But now, he didn't need to tell himself anything at all.

He simply was.

And that was enough.

The older student stood, stretching. "Are you coming to the evening meal?"

The monkey grinned, hopping down from the tree.

"Let's go," he said, his steps feeling lighter than ever.

Pause & Reflect

How often do you believe the stories your mind tells you without questioning them? What happens when you let thoughts come and go—without making them mean something about you?

Chapter 24
The Power of Accepting What Is

The wandering monkey climbed the final stretch of the temple path, his breath steady, his legs working through the familiar ache of the ascent. The morning mist had lifted, revealing the vast valley below, where golden light spilled across the treetops. A river glimmered in the distance, winding its way through the hills like a thread of sparkling diamonds.

He paused, wiping a bead of sweat from his brow. He had walked this path many times before.

But this time, he noticed how once, he would have scowled at the sharp stones beneath his feet, cursed the heat of the morning sun, grumbled at the dust clinging to his fur. He would have muttered that life was unfair, that the climb was needlessly difficult, that the temple should have been built lower on the mountain.

Today, there was no fight within him.

The stones were simply stones. The sun was simply the sun. The path had not changed.

Only *he* had.

Yet, a whisper of discontent that he could not place lingered.

He exhaled, rolling his shoulders as he entered the temple courtyard.

The old master sat on a smooth rock, sharpening a knife against a whetstone. The rhythmic *shhhk, shhhk* of steel meeting stone filled the air. His hands moved slowly, deliberately, as if nothing in the world existed but the steady rhythm of sharpening.

The monkey sat beside him, watching.

"Master," he said after a while, "I do not fight the climb anymore. I do not curse the sun or the dust." He hesitated. "And yet..."

The master did not pause. "And yet?"

The monkey drew a breath. His tail flicked once, then stilled. "Something still feels unsettled within me."

The master lifted the knife, examining its edge, then placed it against the stone once more. "Do you wish things were different?"

The monkey paused. "Not exactly. I just..." He ran a hand over his knee, searching for the right words. "I know I can't change the path, the weather, or the wind. I know they'll be as they are." His brow creased in deep thought. "But there's still a part of me that *wants* things to be easier. A part of me that resists, even though I know better."

The master nodded, still sharpening the blade. "I see." He turned the knife in his hands, the steel catching the light. "And because things were not as you wished, you have chosen to suffer with discontent?"

The monkey's ears twitched. "I didn't *choose* it. It just... *happened*."

The master tilted his head. "Did it?"

The rhythmic scraping of the knife against the stone filled the silence.

The master handed him the knife. "Feel the blade."

The monkey ran his finger carefully along the edge. It was sharp. Precise. Ready.

"Now tell me," the master continued. "Did the blade *wish* to be sharp?"

The monkey frowned. "No... it simply is."

The master nodded and ran the blade against the stone once more. "Yes. And yet, would it be of any use if I resented its dullness instead of sharpening it?"

The monkey's breath slowed.

The master gestured toward the valley below. "The river does not argue with the rocks in its path—it flows around them. The wind does not demand the trees move aside—it weaves through their branches. A bird does not wait for the perfect breeze—it opens its wings and meets the sky as it is."

The monkey's tail curled around his feet as he listened.

Just then, a temple student passed by, carrying a small bundle of firewood. The monkey noticed that the student walked with a slight limp, his right foot dragging ever so slightly.

He had seen this student before. He had once been swift, strong—until an accident had changed him.

The monkey had overheard the story a while ago—a fall from the cliffs, a twisted leg that never fully healed.

The student could no longer run as fast as the others. He would never move the same way again.

And yet, here he was—doing his tasks without hesitation, without complaint.

The monkey watched as the student knelt, arranging the firewood carefully near the temple entrance. His movements were measured, deliberate—not rushed, not strained.

He did not curse his leg.

He did not wish his steps were different.

He simply walked the path before him.

The monkey's chest tightened.

He had spent years of his life resisting—wishing things were different, believing that struggle was proof that something was wrong.

But now, he saw it for what it was.

A sharp knife is not an error. It is simply a knife, honed by friction.

A river does not waste time wishing the rocks were gone. It moves.

A bird does not scold the wind. It flies.

The student did not fight the steps he could no longer take. He simply took the ones that remained.

And wasn't that... freedom?

That old part of the monkey still wanted to protest.

But then something in his chest loosened.

The master placed a hand on his shoulder.

"Suffering is not found in the steepness of the climb, little one. It is found in the wish that it were otherwise."

The monkey looked out at the valley below.

The path had been steep, but it had brought him here. The sun had been hot, but it had passed. The wind had blown dust in his face, but he could still see.

Nothing had changed.

Except *him*.

He stood, brushing the dust from his fur. His legs still ached, and the sun still burned hot upon his back.

But now—there was no resistance.

No wishing.

Only peace.

Pause & Reflect

Where in your life are you wishing things were different, rather than accepting them as they are? What would change if you stopped struggling against reality and simply met life as it is?

Chapter 25
Trusting the Timing

The wandering monkey crouched at the edge of a quiet pond, watching ripples spread as a single dragonfly skimmed across the surface. Its wings shimmered in the golden light, darting forward, pausing, hovering—then suddenly shifting direction again.

The pond was home to a cluster of lotus flowers, their wide green leaves floating serenely on the water. But his eyes were fixed on one thing—the unopened bud at the center, still wrapped tight in its green cocoon.

He had been watching it for days, waiting for it to bloom.

It should have opened by now, he thought. *Why is it taking so long?*

Impatience prickled through him. He had tried coaxing it, nudging the stem, even muttering encouragement.

"Come on, flower! I've seen bananas ripen faster than this. You're doing this on purpose, aren't you?"

But the bud remained closed, untouched by his demands.

With a huff, the monkey flopped onto his back, staring at the sky. His tail twitched against the earth.

"Why does waiting still feel difficult?"

He had learned patience before—*hadn't he?* Yet the urge to hurry things along still crept in.

A voice drifted over from the shaded path.

"Ah, little one. What troubles you now?"

The monkey lifted his head to see the old master walking toward the pond, his robe flowing gently with each step.

The monkey sat up, gesturing toward the lotus. "I've been waiting for this flower to open, but it refuses. I don't understand! The sun is warm, the water is still—what more does it need?"

The master peered at the bud, his face thoughtful. "Ah," he said, "so you believe it should bloom simply because *you* are ready for it?"

The monkey crossed his arms. "Well… yes. If it's going to bloom, why not now?"

The master chuckled and settled beside him, picking up a smooth stone. With a small flick, he tossed it into the pond.

The monkey watched as ripples spread outward, distorting the sky's reflection.

"Tell me," the master said, "does the pond force the ripples to settle?"

The monkey frowned. "…No. They settle on their own."

The master reached toward a small pile of unripe berries resting beside him. He picked one up, rolling it between his fingers.

"And these berries," the master said, "do they sweeten because you demand it?"

The monkey sighed. "No… they ripen when they ripen."

The master nodded. "And the moon—does it rush to meet the night, simply because someone desires to see it?"

The monkey was quiet.

A dragonfly skimmed the water's surface again, never in a hurry, never rushing toward anything. It moved when it moved.

The master held up the berry and gave it a gentle squeeze.

"Pick it too soon, and it is sour. Leave it too long, and it will wither. It ripens exactly when it is ready—and not a moment before."

The monkey released a slow, steady breath, then shook his head. "But what if I miss it? What if the flower blooms when I'm not here?"

The master smiled. "Then it was never yours to witness." He let the berry roll from his palm. "But tell me—do you truly believe life withholds what is meant for you?"

The monkey hesitated.

Had he been treating life like a stubborn tree that refused to bear fruit the moment he was hungry? As if his impatience alone could hurry the ripening of things?

He frowned, echoes of a distant lesson stirring in his mind—the master had once told him that action, taken at the right time, flows effortlessly, but action taken too soon only creates struggle.

Had he forgotten?

The lotus did not resist its own timing, nor did the river force its currents. Wasn't this the same?

The master continued, "The pond does not rush the ripples. The berry does not force itself to ripen. The moon does not fight the night. There is a rhythm to all things. And when you trust it, life unfolds with ease. Things fall into place. Your moment comes—*exactly when it is meant to.*"

The monkey looked at the lotus bud again. It was still closed.

But now, he saw it differently.

What if the waiting was part of the blooming? What if his own unfolding was no different from the flower's?

He sat back, feeling the warmth of the sun, the steady breath of the world, the presence of the master beside him.

Perhaps he was not waiting for the lotus, but with it?

The flower would bloom when it was ready.

And when it did, he would be here—or he wouldn't.

The ripples would settle.

The berry would ripen.

The moon would rise.

And the world would unfold exactly as it was meant to.

Pause & Reflect

Where in your life are you waiting for something to happen, rather than trusting the timing of its unfolding? What if this moment—exactly as it is—is part of what is meant to bloom?

Chapter 26
Beyond Judgment and Duality

The wandering monkey sat at the edge of the riverbank, watching the water move. On one side, the sunlight danced on the rippling surface, golden and warm. On the other, the river ran beneath the shadow of the cliffs, dark and cool.

Same river. Two completely different faces.

He dipped his hand into the light, feeling the warmth. Then into the shade, feeling the chill.

He frowned, as he reflected on the contrast.

Which was better?

Warmth was comforting, but too much of it made him hot and sluggish.

The cool shade was refreshing, but too much of it left him shivering.

He rubbed his chin, deep in thought.

Maybe the warm side is better because it's more inviting.

But the cool side is better when it's too hot outside.

But what if I lived somewhere cold? Then warmth would be more precious.

But then again, if I lived somewhere hot, I'd want the coolness more.

His brow furrowed. His tail flicked.

So which is better?

A familiar voice interrupted his thoughts.

"Ah, little one. You look as though you are trying to decide something."

The monkey turned to see the old master stepping onto the smooth stones of the riverbank.

"Master," the monkey said, staring at the water, "why is there always contrast in things? Warm and cold. Light and dark. Joy and sorrow. It seems as if one always interrupts the other."

The master smiled. "And what would happen, little one, if there were no contrast?"

The monkey blinked. He hadn't thought about that.

He glanced up at the sky.

"If there were no night, we wouldn't need the sun." He picked up a smooth river stone. "If there were no rough edges, how would the water make stones smooth?"

The master knelt beside him, placing a hand in the cool water. "Tell me, is the river flowing because of the water or the rocks beneath it?"

The monkey paused. "Both."

The master nodded. "Without the rocks, the water would be still. Without the water, the rocks would never change. Each shapes the other. The tension between them is what creates the river."

The monkey frowned. "So are opposites... necessary?"

The master picked up a handful of pebbles and let them slip through his fingers.

"What would laughter mean if you had never known sorrow? What would rest mean if you had never felt tired? If the world were only one thing, could you even recognize it?"

The monkey looked at the river again. The sunlight shimmered on the surface, but only because of the shadow beside it.

Then, across in the garden, he noticed two temple students working in the soil—one carefully tending to a row of herbs, the other struggling to pull a stubborn weed from the ground.

The second student grumbled, yanking at the plant. "This weed is ruining the garden."

The first student smiled, patting the soil around the basil. "But isn't the weed just another plant?"

The monkey's ears twitched. That was an interesting thought.

He turned to the master. "Master, isn't a weed just a plant in the wrong place?"

The master smiled. "Or perhaps, it is only we who decide where a plant belongs."

The monkey frowned. "But some things are good and bad, aren't they? A lush garden is good. A garden full of weeds is bad. Sweet fruit is good. Rotten fruit is bad. Isn't that just... how things are?"

The master gestured for the monkey to follow him toward the students.

"Tell me, little one," the master said, picking up a smooth stone. "If I place this stone in a river, what is it?"

The monkey shrugged. "Just a stone."

The master nodded and placed the stone on the pathway instead. "And here?"

The monkey hesitated. "Still a stone."

The master chuckled. "Ah, but what if a traveler trips over it? Then it is an obstacle. And what if a builder needs it for a wall? Then it is useful."

He turned to the monkey. "Did the stone change? Or did our judgment of it change?"

The monkey's tail flicked as he considered this.

The master continued. "We call something bad when we perceive it does not serve us. We call something good when it pleases us. But the stone, the weed, the rain, the wind—none of them are either. They simply are."

The monkey watched as the second student finally pulled the weed from the soil and tossed it aside. But now, a butterfly landed on its leaves, drinking from the tiny white flowers that were its blooms.

Was it a weed?

Or was it simply another part of the garden?

The master followed his gaze. "You see, little one, we are always looking for the 'better' side of things. But duality is not something to escape. It is what gives life its meaning."

The monkey thought back to the river—the warm light, the cool shade.

He had always been trying to hold on to the good and avoid the bad.

But what if neither was wrong?

What if each simply gave shape to the other?

The master smiled. "And what happens when you stop judging? When you stop deciding what should be?"

The monkey was quiet.

He glanced back at the butterfly resting on the "weed."

"When we stop judging," the master continued, "we stop limiting what something can become."

The monkey looked at him, not quite understanding.

"When you name something as bad, you close the door to its potential. When you decide something is good, you become attached to keeping it that way. But when you stop dividing the world into categories, you step into the greatest freedom."

The monkey let out a slow breath, feeling an old resistance unfurl.

Not everything had to be named.
Not everything had to be controlled.

When he did not judge, he saw more. Possibilities stretched open where limitations had once been.

The master smiled. "And that, little one, is the gift of duality—not in judging and choosing one side over the other, but in seeing that neither side can exist without the other."

The monkey nodded, his chest feeling light.

The river continued to flow, the butterfly continued to sip from the tiny white flowers, and the garden—whether full of weeds or not—was simply the way of life.

And the monkey simply let it.

Pause & Reflect

Where in your life do you find yourself labeling things as "good" or "bad"? What would happen if you stopped trying to choose between opposites, and simply let them be?

Chapter 27
Becoming Empty

The wandering monkey had been helping around the temple, even teaching a few lessons to some of the younger students. That evening, when lessons were over, he sat at the edge of a quiet stream, rolling a smooth stone between his fingers. The late afternoon sun shimmered on the water, golden ripples moving lazily over scattered pebbles. The sweet smell of wild jasmine drifted in waves with the breeze.

He breathed in deeply, filling his lungs, taking it all in.

Was this heaven on earth?

And then—

There it was.

Not frustration. Not confusion.

But *space*.

An awareness of something missing.

Or rather—an awareness of *where something used to be.*

He had spent years chasing wisdom, gathering lessons, searching for answers. His mind had once been a storm of thoughts, spinning endlessly with questions, doubts, and the desperate need to understand.

But now...

It was quiet.

Lighter.

He ran his fingers along the stone, then dropped it into the river and watched the way the water flowed around it, effortless and clear.

This is different.

A familiar voice interrupted his thoughts.

"Ah, little one. You are not troubled, yet you are deep in thought."

The monkey looked up to see the old master stepping carefully over the rocks, his robe brushing against the moss. He carried a small, empty clay bowl in one hand.

The monkey gestured vaguely toward the stream. "I was just thinking, Master. About how... different my mind feels."

The master settled beside him, dipping his fingers into the cool water. "How so?"

The monkey hesitated. "For so long, my mind was *full*—always questioning, always running in circles, always trying to hold onto every lesson, every realization. I thought wisdom was something to collect. That the more I gathered, the wiser I'd become."

He let out a quiet laugh, shaking his head. "But now, it feels... *empty.*"

The master turned the clay bowl over in his hands. "And does this emptiness trouble you?"

The monkey frowned, contemplating. "No... not trouble. It's just *strange*. I don't feel lost, or restless, or weighed down by thoughts like before. I've learned how to let things go. But now, I wonder... *what remains?*"

The master smiled, lifting the empty bowl. "Ah, little one. You have learned to *let go*. And now, you are ready to *become empty*."

The monkey tilted his head. "But haven't I already done that? I've let go of so much."

The master chuckled. "Letting go is the first step. But true emptiness is not just releasing what you no longer need. It is no longer feeling the need to hold at all."

The monkey's ears twitched. Not long ago, he would have scoffed at such an idea. Or panicked at it.

Now, he simply sat with it.

The master tapped the side of the bowl lightly. "Tell me, little one. Is an empty bowl useless?"

The monkey shook his head.

The master turned the bowl again. "And does it struggle to be filled?"

The monkey's lips twitched into a small smile. "No. It simply waits."

The master nodded. "Yes. Because an empty bowl is not lacking—it is *ready*."

The monkey ran his fingers along the stone beside him, feeling its cool surface. "But why does this emptiness feel so... peaceful?"

The master's eyes gleamed. "Because, little one, when you are empty, you are finally *at rest*."

The monkey frowned slightly. "*At rest?*"

The master placed the bowl down gently. "Tell me, do you remember when your mind was always full?"

The monkey laughed out loud. "How could I forget?"

The master chuckled. "And when your mind was full, tell me—did you ever feel at peace?"

The monkey paused.

He thought back to the restless days, the endless questions. The need to hold onto everything. To *figure everything out*.

He thought back to how exhausting it had all been.

"No," he admitted. "I was always searching for something. Always chasing."

The master nodded. "And now?"

The monkey looked at the river, at how effortlessly it moved. At how it *allowed*.

"I'm not searching anymore," he said softly.

The master smiled. "That is peace, little one."

They sat in silence, watching the stream carry leaves gently downstream, the water neither holding nor resisting.

The monkey took a deep breath, feeling the stillness settle inside him.

This was not the emptiness of losing something.

This was the emptiness of *needing nothing*.

The bowl beside him remained empty.

And for the first time in his life—

So did he.

But now, emptiness did not feel like the absence of something—

It felt like the beginning of everything.

Pause & Reflect

Where in your life are you still holding on—whether to thoughts, expectations, or identities? What might happen if you emptied your cup and became open to something new?

Chapter 28
The Dance of Sovereignty

The monkey danced through the trees, his movements light, effortless, as if he were carried by the wind itself.

He no longer climbed as a seeker, reaching for something just beyond grasp.

He no longer wandered, restless and uncertain.

He was simply *here*.

Present. Whole.

The jungle pulsed with life around him—birds bursting into song, leaves whispering in the breeze, the sun dappling golden patterns across the forest floor.

Once, he would have rushed past all of this, lost in thoughts of where he should be, who he should become.

But today, he moved not with urgency, but with joy.

No longer the *wandering* monkey.

Now, the *dancing* monkey.

At the edge of the clearing, the old master sat beneath a sprawling banyan tree, his eyes half-closed, listening to the rustling world.

The monkey approached, a smile playing on his lips.

The master opened his eyes. "Ah, little one. I see something has changed."

The monkey nodded, dropping onto the soft earth beside him. "I used to believe I had to find something, Master. That wisdom was somewhere *out there*, waiting for me to catch up to it."

The master chuckled. "And now?"

The monkey stretched his arms wide, feeling the sunlight warm his skin. "Now I see... there was nothing to *find*. Only something to *realize*."

The master nodded approvingly. "And what is different?"

The monkey thought for a moment. "I used to feel like I had to *fix* myself. Like I was always on the verge of becoming something better, something *more*. Always reaching, always waiting for the moment when I would finally be... enough. But now, I don't feel like I need to change anything. I was never missing. I was never incomplete."

The master smiled. "Ah, now you understand."

He picked up a small stone and tossed it lightly into the air. It turned and spun before landing softly in his palm. "The stone is no less perfect for being tossed. The river is no less whole for moving. And you, little one, were never incomplete."

The monkey watched the leaves swaying above, shifting in the light. "So all my seeking—everything I thought I needed to learn—was never about becoming something else."

The master nodded. "It was about *remembering* what you already are."

A quiet stillness settled between them. Then, from within his robe, the master pulled out a single feather. He held it up, letting it catch the breeze. The feather twisted, turned, floated—yet it did not *belong* to him.

"Sovereignty in consciousness, little one, is knowing that you are the *sky*—not the weather that moves through it. You may hear voices, opinions, doubts… but they do not define you. You are not required to chase them or believe them."

The monkey held the feather, watching how effortlessly it moved with the wind.

He thought of all the moments he had been swayed by others' ideas, by expectations, by the fear of making the wrong choice.

Perhaps sovereignty was never about silencing the voices, nor about proving them wrong.

It was about knowing which voice was truly his.

The thoughts, the doubts, the need to grasp at meaning… they had always been passing clouds.

But he?

He was the sky they drifted through.

Untouched. Unchanged.

He was not his doubts.
He was not the opinions of others.
He was not the passing fears of the moment.

He was the presence beneath them all.

A deep peace settled over him, not as an idea, but as something *felt*.

He had spent so long chasing after meaning, after purpose, after understanding.

But all along, life had been happening. *Right here. Right now.*

No effort. No struggle. No need to grasp or strive.

The master reached out, gently brushing a fallen leaf from the monkey's shoulder.

"You see, little one, sovereignty is not about *control*. It is not about *mastering* life. It is about *dancing with it*."

The monkey laughed softly. "That's it, isn't it? It's all a dance."

The master nodded. "A dance of experience, of awareness, of *being*. And when you stop trying to lead—when you *trust* the rhythm—you will always move in harmony."

The monkey rose to his feet, stretching toward the sky. He stepped forward, surprised at how light he felt.

No weight, no burden—just movement.

The world was no longer a puzzle to solve, no longer a path to follow.

It was simply something to *dance with*.

With a playful grin, he leapt into the trees, his movements fluid, effortless, alive.

The wind carried him, the branches swayed beneath his touch.

He no longer reached for something unseen.

He no longer *reached* at all.

He simply *moved*.

As the river flows.

As the wind shifts.

As the stars appear in the endless sky, neither rushing nor resisting.

And in that moment—

He was not just *in* the infinite sky.

He *was* the sky.

Pause & Reflect

Have you ever mistaken passing thoughts or fears for the truth of who you are? How does it feel to imagine yourself as the sky, with thoughts passing like clouds?

☐ **The Dance of Coming Home** – One more story—the final conversation between the monkey and the master can be downloaded with the other offerings to help deepen your journey here:

https://bonuses.serenachoo.com/monkey-zen-unlock-your-bonuses/ or scan the QR code below.

These gifts are yours. May they remind you of the stillness beneath the noise, the space between the stories, and the infinite sky within.

Stay A Moment Longer

Come, sit for a while.

There is no rush. No urgency.

There is no ending—only this moment.

Like the wandering monkey, you have walked through many stories, each one offering a glimpse of something deeper. But wisdom is not something to collect, nor is peace something to chase. It is already here, within you, waiting to be seen.

There is nothing to fix. Nothing to force.

You do not need to have all the answers.

Life is not a puzzle to solve, but a dance to be moved through—sometimes with ease, sometimes with challenge, always unfolding exactly as it should.

So take a breath.

Let go of striving.

Trust the rhythm of life.

And when the moment calls—

Leap.

Share Your Reflection

If *The Monkey and the Way of Zen* touched you, offered a moment of stillness, or sparked a new perspective, I'd be deeply grateful if you shared your experience with others.

Your review is more than words—it's a ripple that helps fellow readers discover this book when they might need it most. It also guides me in creating offerings that continue to serve and inspire.

Even a few lines can make a meaningful difference.

There are just 3 steps:

1. Log into your Amazon account

2. Click on "Returns & Orders" to access your orders

3. Find this book *The Monkey and the Way of Zen* in your orders, then click on "Write a product review."

Thank you for being part of this journey. May the wisdom you carry from these pages continue to unfold in your life.

A Note From the Author: Where This Book Meets Buddhist Psychology

The Monkey and the Way of Zen is not a traditional Buddhist psychology text, but many of its themes overlap. The wandering monkey's journey mirrors the way the mind clings, resists, and struggles—only to discover that peace is found in surrender, presence, and letting go.

For readers who found this book while exploring Buddhist psychology, you may recognize reflections of core teachings:

☐ **Perception Shapes Reality** – Suffering arises not from what happens, but from how the mind relates to it. Shifts in perception shift experience.

☐ **Letting Go of Attachment** – The monkey clings to control, certainty, and "answers"—but freedom arrives only through release.

☐ **The Illusion of Self** – What we call "self" is rarely solid. The monkey's path is less about discovery, more about unlearning who he thought he was.

☐ **The Power of the Present Moment** – The master returns him again and again to the now. Not through instruction, but through quiet nudges toward awareness.

☐ **Beyond the Thinking Mind** – At some point, words fall away. Understanding comes not from analysis, but from a deeper, felt knowing.

This book wasn't written to teach these ideas, but as a doorway to embodying them—lightly, through story. If something in it resonated with you, that's more than I could wish for.

May the stories leave a gentle imprint—one that invites you home to the wisdom already within.

About the Author

Serena Choo is a lifelong reader, storyteller, and questioner of the bigger picture. She wrote *The Monkey and the Way of Zen* in honor of her Chinese heritage and a family lineage of royal scholars and officials.

A polymath by nature, she is always learning, always refining—absorbing and distilling insights from diverse fields and perspectives. With an innate ability to meet people exactly where they are, she transforms complexity into understanding, bridging intellect and intuition. Her works are a reflection of this depth, a glimpse into the vast reservoir she draws from.

Serena believes that stories have the power to shift perspectives and reveal the quiet truths we often overlook. Her work invites readers to discover not just ideas but to awaken to the deeper awareness that underlies everyday experience.

Through *The Monkey and the Way of Zen*, Serena shares an invitation: to pause, to breathe, and to rediscover the simplicity and freedom that have always been within reach.

You can explore more of her writings and upcoming projects at: serenachoo.com or scan the QR code for her Author page on Amazon.